A COURSE IN ATTIC GREEK, I

1. The Parthenon, as viewed from the Athenian Acropolis,
dedicated in 438 BC to the goddess Athena.

A COURSE IN ATTIC GREEK, I

James K. Finn
and
Frank J. Groton, Jr.

Revised & Expanded by
Patrick G. Lake

4th Edition

The Hill School
Pottstown, Pennsylvania
2012

FOURTH EDITION
ISBN: 978-1-300-05112-1
PRINTED IN THE UNITED STATES OF AMERICA

To the students of The Hill School

CONTENTS

PREFACE

A knowledge of Greek thought and life, and of the arts in which the Greeks expressed their thought and sentiment, is essential to high culture. A man may know everything else, but without this knowledge he remains ignorant of the best intellectual and moral achievement of the human race.

Charles Eliot Norton

This book is a revision of the first half of *A Basic Course for Reading Attic Greek*, a text first conceived of and written in the summer of 1978 by Frank J. Groten, Jr. and my former colleague James K. Finn, to be used in The Hill School's beginning and intermediate Greek courses. This new text has preserved the order of presentation in the original text, its vocabulary, and the vast majority of its drills and exercises. All grammatical explanations, however, have been clarified and in most cases completely rewritten. The paradigm charts have been reformatted and in most cases now include a translation of the form as well as the form itself. These forms are now collected for easy reference in the Appendices in the back of the text. The number and quality of figures and illustrations have been augmented significantly. There is now an index for all verb principal parts. There is no delay, moreover, in the introduction of all principal parts of the verb. This new text also explains all grammatical concepts in detail, such as aspect, voice, and so on, with an eye towards the beginning student for whom such material is thoroughly foreign. Even more so than the previous edition, this text places a heavy emphasis on the explanation of euphonic change in Greek, with the assumption that a student who understands the principles behind euphonic change will be more likely to master his forms and hence the language itself. The final addition to this new text: all lessons have been augmented with additional drill work, in most cases two new drills per lesson.

As in the original text, two contrasting methods of presentation of the material have been considered: the one, inductive, offering a series of reading selections with lexical items, form and constructions appended, and the other, deductive, based on a text that leads to selections illustrating linguistic materials explained previously. By the former method a student must rely virtually from the beginning upon a formidable array of supplementary vocabulary and syntactical notes, whereas the latter, as used in this text, presupposes the mastery of fundamentals which have been introduced and reinforced before a reading occurs.

Since the effectiveness of this "traditional" approach depends entirely upon the logic, accuracy, and clarity with which the lexical items and grammar are organized and presented, great care has been taken with the choice of Greek words and with the arrangement of paradigms and grammatical descriptions. Vocabulary and linguistic patterns are systematically repeated in various exercises so that they are mastered before a passage of connected prose is encountered.

This text is focused on grammar, reading, and composition. While the text is not designed to offer a synthesis of the Greek experience or a description of daily life in ancient Athens, the readings and sentences have been selected in such a way that they offer a gateway to discussions about Greek literature, history, and culture.

Listed below are some additional criteria observed in the composition of this text:

1. The text presupposes the mastery of no other foreign language, including Latin.

2. All grammatical points are fully explained in the text and illustrated by examples so that the student can assimilate independently what has been presented in class.

3. The rules of accentuation are introduced gradually and only as needed in order not to confuse the beginner with material unfamiliar to him.

4. So that the student is not overwhelmed by the task of memorization, each lesson's vocabulary list is limited to approximately ten words. Common English derivatives, where appropriate, are provided.

5. A number behind each entry in the Greek-English and English-Greek vocabularies in the rear of the primer indicates the lesson in which each word has been introduced.

6. The Greek sentences in each lesson are formulated in such a way that they repeatedly illustrate vocabulary and constructions in stimulating contexts, since many have been derived from significant ideas and events in Greek literature.

7. After the tenth lesson, review lessons occur about every five lessons.

8. In keeping with the authors' belief that Greek composition remains an essential exercise in the thorough mastery of vocabulary and idiom, develops analytical habits by requiring close attention to detail, and encourages creativity by demanding the practical implementation of acquired knowledge and skills, considerable emphasis is placed upon the translation of English sentences into Greek.

9. Particular attention is devoted to the relative frequency of Greek forms; thus the aorist tense and the middle voice are introduced in early lessons since they are so common, while the future passive participle, certain moods of the perfect (subjunctive, optative, imperative) as well as the future perfect system, and all dual forms are introduced very late and then only in a supplementary context because they occur so infrequently in Greek.

Thanks are owed to my colleague Henry V. Bender, for his encouragement in the pursuit of this project and Headmaster David Dougherty for his support of the Classics generally at The Hill School. Finally, many thanks to those students who patiently endured earlier drafts of this textbook, especially Berenger Wegman, Cameron Isen, Youngweon Lee, Jennifer Schmitt, and Braden Cordivari for identifying many typographical errors.

The Hill School   Patrick G. Lake, Ph. D.
Pottstown, Pennsylvania
June, 2012

Lesson 1

The Greek Alphabet and its Pronunciation

Alphabet

Character Lower / Upper		Name	Pronunciation	English Transliteration
α	A	alpha	dr<u>a</u>m<u>a</u>	a
β	B	beta	<u>b</u>ut	b
γ	Γ	gamma	<u>g</u>o	g
δ	Δ	delta	<u>d</u>o	d
ε	E	epsilon	<u>e</u>pic	e
ζ	Z	zeta	<u>z</u>one	z
η	H	eta	<u>ei</u>ght	ē
θ	Θ	theta	<u>th</u>eater	th
ι	I	iota	<u>i</u>ntr<u>i</u>gue	i
κ	K	kappa	<u>k</u>in, <u>c</u>ard	k, c
λ	Λ	lambda	<u>l</u>ip	l
μ	M	mu	<u>m</u>ap	m
ν	N	nu	<u>n</u>o	n
ξ	Ξ	xi	a<u>x</u>is	x
ο	O	omicron	<u>ou</u>ght	o
π	Π	pi	<u>p</u>ick	p
ρ	P	rho	fai<u>r</u>, <u>rh</u>ythm	r, rh (ῥ)
σ,ς	Σ	sigma	<u>s</u>it	s
τ	T	tau	<u>t</u>ea	t
υ	Y	upsilon	d<u>u</u>tif<u>u</u>l	y, u
φ	Φ	phi	<u>ph</u>ase	ph
χ	X	chi	<u>ch</u>aracter	ch
ψ	Ψ	psi	la<u>ps</u>e	ps
ω	Ω	omega	<u>o</u>cean	ō

Notes

When γ occurs before another γ or before κ, χ, or ξ, it is pronounced like the "n" in "sink." Examples: ἀνάγκη (anankē), ἄγγελος (angelos).

Final sigma (ς) is written only at the end of a word. Example: σοφός.

Diphthongs

By definition, a diphthong is a combination of vowels pronounced as a single sound. For example, in English the "ei" in "reiterate" is not a diphthong – the vowels "e" and "i" belong to different syllables – but the "ei" in "receive" is a dipthong as the vowels "e" and "i" are part of the same syllable.

Diphthongs	Pronunciation	Transliteration
αι	aisle	e, ae
αυ	sauerkraut	au
ει	eight	i, e, ei
ου	group	u
ευ	"ε" + "ου"	eu
ηυ	"η" + "ου"	eu
οι	oil	i, e, oi, oe
υι	suite	ui

Diacritical Marks: Breathings and Accents

The Hellenistic era (c. 323-146 BC), which followed the conquests of Alexander the Great, was characterized by the spread of Greek language and culture throughout a large area of Europe, Asia, and Africa. During this time, diacritical marks were added to Greek to ensure proper pronunciation of the language by foreigners. Two breathing marks were added: a rough breathing (῾), pronounced like the letter "h," and a smooth breathing (᾿), which indicated the absence of an "h" sound. All initial vowel sounds and initial rho (ρ) in Greek receive breathing marks. Examples:

Rough: ὑπέρ (hyper); Ὅμηρος (Homēros)
Smooth: ἀνήρ (anēr); Εὐριπίδης (Euripidēs)

Note that breathing marks are written <u>above</u> lowercase characters and <u>to the left</u> of uppercase characters. In the case of diphthongs, like the Εὐ of Εὐριπίδης, the breathing is written over the final vowel of the diphthong. In Greek, <u>initial</u> ρ and υ always receive a rough breathing (e.g. ῥήτωρ, rhētōr).

Greek employs three different accent marks: the acute (´), grave (` ), and circumflex ( ^ ). As ancient Greek employed a pitch accent, originally these accents indicated pitch changes: an acute ( ´ ) indicated a rise in pitch, the grave ( `) a fall, and the circumflex (^) both a rise and a fall. Today is it common practice to render the pitch accent of ancient Greek as a stress accent, the ordinary system of accentuation in English.

Drill A

Write the upper and lower case Greek character:

1. mu	9. upsilon	17. rho
2. beta	10. gamma	18. epsilon
3. omicron	11. omega	19. psi
4. zeta	12. kappa	20. iota
5. chi	13. phi	21. xi
6. alpha	14. theta	22. nu
7. sigma	15. tau	23. lambda
8. eta	16. delta	24. pi

Drill B

Pronounce the following Greek words, stressing the accented syllable. Write an English word that is derived from each Greek word:

1. ἀθλητής	11. ἀστρονομία	21. δόγμα
2. ἄγγελος	12. μαθηματικός	22. βάρβαρος
3. τεχνικός	13. ἀναισθησία	23. κινητικός
4. πνευμονία	14. μίμησις	24. βιβλίον
5. ἄγκυρα	15. ἄσβεστος	25. φυσικός
6. ἁρμονία	16. σχολή	26. γεωμετρία
7. πολιτικός	17. ἀριθμητικός	27. θεολογία
8. ἱστορία	18. μικροφωνία	28. μηχανικός
9. βιογραφία	19. γυμναστικός	29. διάγραμμα
10. φαινόμενον	20. ἀναρχία	30. φιλοσοφία

Drill C

Transliterate, using both uppercase and lowercase Greek characters:

1. basis
2. drama
3. hypokritēs
4. climax
5. crisis
6. arōma
7. diplōma
8. skeleton
9. charactēr
10. nemesis
11. zōnē
12. chaos
13. mētropolis
14. genesis
15. amnēsia
16. rhododendron
17. pneumonia
18. analysis

Drill D

Write out the following Greek words in both upper and lower case characters. Write an English word that is derived from each Greek word:

1. pi omicron iota epsilon omega
2. phi rho alpha zeta omega
3. delta epsilon sigma pi omicron tau eta sigma
4. rho eta tau omega rho
5. chi alpha rho mu alpha
6. sigma tau alpha delta iota omicron nu
7. delta epsilon kappa alpha
8. gamma rho alpha mu mu alpha
9. phi alpha rho mu alpha kappa omicron nu
10. delta upsilon omicron

2. The Theater of Dionysius, on the south slope of the Acropolis, Athens.

Lesson 2

Present Active Indicative and Infinitive

Tense, Voice, and Mood

All verbs possess tense, voice, and mood. Tense denotes the "time" of the verb, that is to say whether the verb describes a present, past, or future action. Voice is used to describe the relationship between the verb and its subject. In the active voice, the subject does the action of the verb (e.g. I (subject) throw (verb) the ball (object)). In the passive voice, the subject receives the action of the verb (e.g. The ball (subject) is thrown (verb)). Mood denotes the basic "mode" of the verb. The indicative mood, for example, states facts (e.g. I am writing), while the imperative mood is used for direct commands (e.g. Write, scholars!).

Most verbs also have person and number. Person and number are used to specify the subject of the verb. The first person in the singular is "I"; in the plural, it is "we." The second person is "you," in the singular and the plural. The third person is "he," "she," or "it" in the singular, "they" in the plural. The infinitive mood is so-called because it is "infinite" in the sense that it is not limited by a person or number. Rather than "he educated," the present infinitive, for example, simply expresses the idea "to educate."

ω-Verbs

There are two types or conjugations of verbs in Greek: ω-verbs and μι-verbs. This chapter will introduce the more common conjugation, ω-verbs; μι-verbs will be introduced later in the second volume of this text, *A Course in Attic Greek*, II (see Lesson 52). Verbs in Greek are divided into conjugation types because each conjugation type generally has a different way of creating the various forms of the verb.

The Present Active Indicative and Infinitive

The present active indicative for ω-verbs is formed by adding an ending to the present stem. The present stem is found by dropping the -ω from the end of the first principal part of the verb. Example:

Principal parts: παιδεύω (*I educate*), παιδεύσω (*I will educate*), ἐπαίδευσα (*I educated*), πεπαίδευκα (*I have educated*), πεπαίδευμαι (*I have educated myself* or *I have been educated*), ἐπαιδεύθην (*I was educated*)
Present stem: παιδεύ-

Principal parts – like those of the verb παιδεύω above – are the basic building blocks of the verb, providing the various stems for all of the verb's different forms. In English, for example, verbs typically have three principal parts. Examples:

      eat, ate, eaten

      sing, sang, sung

In Greek, verbs typically have six principal parts. The first principal part provides the stem for all of the verb's present tense forms.

In the chart below, the present stem is separated from the ending by a dash. The ending itself for an ω-verb like παιδεύω is made up of two parts: a thematic vowel and a personal ending. In most forms of the present active indicative, the thematic vowel and the personal ending are blended together. This is not the case, however, in the first person plural and the second person plural, where an additional dash is used in the chart below to separate the thematic vowel from the personal ending.

<u>singular</u>	<u>person</u>	<u>plural</u>
παιδεύ-ω	1	παιδεύ-ο-μεν
I educate		*We educate*
παιδεύ-εις	2	παιδεύ-ε-τε
You educate		*You educate*
παιδεύ-ει	3	παιδεύ-ουσι(ν)
He / She / It educates		*They educate*

Infinitive   παιδεύ-ειν

              to be educating

Note: The translations used in the chart above are in the <u>simple present</u> ("I educate"). The present active indicative can also be translated, given the appropriate context, using the <u>progressive present</u> ("I am educating") or the <u>emphatic present</u> ("I do educate").

ν-Movable

The (ν) at the end of the third person plural form παιδεύουσι above is called ν-movable. A ν is typically added to the end of the third person plural of the present active indicative in Greek, when this form appears at the end of a clause or when it is followed by a word beginning with a vowel. This latter situation – a word ending in a vowel followed by one beginning with a vowel – is known as hiatus, a situation that Greek, like English, tends to avoid. English avoids hiatus by using the indefinite article "an" before words beginning with a vowel, as in "<u>an</u> encyclopedia" rather than "<u>a</u> encyclopedia."

Accented Syllables

Only the final three syllables of a Greek word may receive an accent. These syllables are named as follows:

παι – δεύ – ω
antepenult – penult – ultima

The length of these syllables determines where the accent falls, with the length of the <u>ultima</u> of primary importance. Syllable length, for the purposes of accentuation, is determined by the quantity of the vowels that make up the syllable. Vowel quantity is determined as follows:

<u>Always short</u>	<u>Always long</u>	<u>Long or short</u>
ε	η	α
ο	ω	ι
	diphthongs	υ

<u>Note</u>: The iota (ι) of the third person plural ending (-ουσι(ν)) is short.

Verbs in Greek, with the exception of participles, employ a "recessive accent," meaning that the accent will be placed as far towards the beginning of the verb as possible, as determined primarily by the length of the ultima as follows:

<u>For all verbs</u>
Acute
[penult] [<u>long</u> ultima]   παι[δεύ][ω]   ἐ[θέλ][εις]

<u>For verbs of three or more syllables</u>
  Acute
[antepenult] [penult] [<u>short</u> ultima]   παι[δεύ][ο][μεν]   [ἄ][γου][σιν]

<u>For verbs of only two syllables</u>
  Acute
[<u>short</u> penult] [short ultima]   [ἔσ][χον]   [γράφ][ε]

Circumflex
[<u>long</u> penult] [short ultima]   [ἦ][χε]   [εἶ][λον]

<u>Note</u>: The use of the grave accent will be treated in Lesson 3.

Punctuation

Greek uses four punctuation marks: the period (.), the comma (,), the colon or semicolon (·), and the question mark (;).

Vocabulary

ἄγω, ἄξω, ἤγαγον, ἦχα, ἦγμαι, ἤχθην *lead, bring* (pedagogue)

βλάπτω, βλάψω, ἔβλαψα, βέβλαφα, βέβλαμμαι, ἐβλάφθην (ἐβλάβην) *harm, hurt*

γράφω, γράψω, ἔγραψα, γέγραφα, γέγραμμαι, ἐγράφην *write* (graphite)

διαφθείρω, διαφθερῶ, διέφθειρα, διέφθαρκα, διέφθαρμαι, διεφθάρην *corrupt, ruin*

ἐθέλω, ἐθελήσω, ἠθέλησα, ἠθέληκα, ____, ____ *wish, be willing*

κλέπτω, κλέψω, ἔκλεψα, κέκλοφα, κέκλεμμαι, ἐκλάπην *steal* (cleptomaniac)

παιδεύω, παιδεύσω, ἐπαίδευσα, πεπαίδευκα, πεπαίδευμαι, ἐπαιδεύθην *educate*

σπεύδω, σπεύσω, ἔσπευσα, ____, ____, ____ *hasten, hurry*

Note: The English words in *italics* denote English meanings for the Greek; those in parentheses () denote English derivatives from the Greek. Throughout the textbook, vocabulary will be arranged alphabetically by part of speech.

Drill A

Conjugate and translate the verbs below in the present active indicative, accenting all forms properly:

      1. ἄγω   2. γράφω

Drill B

Write the name of the underlined syllables (antepenult, penult, ultima):

    1. ἀγα<u>θός</u>   4. <u>υἱ</u>οι
    2. διαφ<u>θεί</u>ρουσι   5. <u>ἔ</u>χουσι
    3. θε<u>οῦ</u>   6. <u>νό</u>σον

Drill C

Translate and parse the following verb forms (<u>Note</u>: To parse a verb, identify its tense, voice, mood and, if finite, its person and number):

1. γράφουσι
2. ἐθέλειν
3. ἄγομεν
4. διαφθείρετε
5. κλέπτεις

6. σπεύδειν
7. παιδεύει
8. βλάπτετε
9. διαφθείρω
10. ἄγουσι

Drill D

Translate into Greek, accenting all forms properly:

1. We corrupt
2. They are writing
3. You (sg.) do harm
4. We are educating
5. He does steal

6. You (sg.) are leading
7. Am I willing to hasten?
8. We bring
9. Does he hurry?
10. Are you (pl.) willing to steal?

3. ὁ Σωκράτης παιδεύει.

Lesson 3

Masculine Nouns of the Second Declension
Nominative Subject and Accusative Direct Object

Gender

Greek nouns have gender: masculine, feminine, or neuter. The gender of a noun does not have an effect on its translation or meaning; it is merely a grammatical category, of particular importance for the agreement of adjectives and other modifiers. This chapter will treat only nouns of the masculine gender.

Case Uses: Nominative Subject and Accusative Direct Object

Greek is an inflected language, meaning that the forms of words change to indicate their function in a sentence. English also has some inflection, albeit little compared to Greek. Consider, for example, the way the pronoun "he" changes to reflect its function in a sentence:

Form	Function	Case
He likes to learn Greek.	Subject	Nominative
Greek is his favorite subject.	Possession	Genitive
I teach it to him.	Indirect Object	Dative
Greek challenges him.	Direct Object	Accusative

As the chart above indicates, the form and function of a word in Greek are characterized by a "case." The chart above is a gross simplification of how cases operate in Greek; in practice, a case like the accusative case, for example, can do more than indicate the direct object of a sentence. This lesson, however, will focus only on the most basic uses of the nominative and accusative cases, as subject and direct object respectively. Example:

$$\text{ὁ ἄνθρωπος ἄγει τὸν ἵππον.}$$
The man is leading the horse.
(nominative subject)   /   (accusative direct object)

The Second Declension

In the same way that verbs in Greek belong to a certain conjugation (either -ω or -μι), Greek nouns belong to the first, second, or third declension. Each declension has characteristic case endings.

A second declension noun is identified by the presence of an -ου ending in the genitive singular form, listed in the vocabulary as follows:

Vocabulary entry: ἄνθρωπος, -ου, ὁ *man*

Dropping the -ου from the genitive singular provides the noun's stem:

Noun stem: ἄνθρωπ-

In the chart below, the stem is separated from the case ending by a dash.

	singular		plural
ὁ ἄνθρωπ-ος	Nominative	οἱ ἄνθρωπ-οι	
(the) man		*(the) men*	
τοῦ ἀνθρώπ-ου	Genitive	τῶν ἀνθρώπ-ων	
of (the) man		*of (the) men*	
τῷ ἀνθρώπ-ῳ	Dative	τοῖς ἀνθρώπ-οις	
to/for (the) man		*to/for (the) men*	
τὸν ἄνθρωπ-ον	Accusative	τοὺς ἀνθρώπ-ους	
(the) man		*(the) men*	

The Definite Article

The chart above also shows the declension of the masculine definite article, ὁ. The definite article may be translated into English as "the." Sometimes it is best ignored in translation, however, since Greek uses the article differently than English. In Greek, for example, the article typically appears with abstract nouns. It may not be best, however, given the context to translate a sentence like ἡ ἀρετή ἐστὶ ἀγαθὸς as *the virtue is good* rather than simply *virtue is good.* As an additional idiomatic caveat: the Greek definite article is sometimes best translated into English as a possessive pronoun ("my," "your," "his," etc.) to indicate possession by the subject. Example:

ὁ ἄνθρωπος παιδεύει τὸν υἱόν.
The man is educating his son.

Persistent Accent

Unlike verbs, nouns, in addition to adjectives and participles in Greek, employ a "persistent accent," meaning that the accent tends to stay or "persist" on the syllable on which it appears in the nominative singular. Like verbs, the length of the ultima is of primary importance for determining the position and type of the accent for nouns. The nominative plural ending -οι is considered to be short for the purposes of accentuation. Different classes of nouns in the second declension are accented as follows:

<u>Acute Accent on the Antepenult in the Nominative Singular</u>

singular		plural
ὁ θάνατος	Nom.	οἱ θάνατοι
τοῦ θανά<u>του</u>	Gen.	τῶν θανά<u>των</u>
τῷ θανά<u>τῳ</u>	Dat.	τοῖς θανά<u>τοις</u>
τὸν θάνατον	Acc.	τοὺς θανά<u>τους</u>

<u>Note</u>: The accent moves to the penult when there is a <u>long ultima</u>.

<u>Acute Accent on a Short Penult in the Nominative Singular</u>

singular		plural
ὁ φίλος	Nom.	οἱ φίλοι
τοῦ φίλου	Gen.	τῶν φίλων
τῷ φίλῳ	Dat.	τοῖς φίλοις
τὸν φίλον	Acc.	τοὺς φίλους

<u>Note</u>: The accent does not move or change its type. An example of an acute accent on a <u>long</u> penult will appear in Lesson 7.

<u>Acute Accent on the Ultima in the Nominative Singular</u>

singular		plural
ὁ ἀδελφός	Nom.	οἱ ἀδελφοί
τοῦ ἀδελφοῦ	Gen.	τῶν ἀδελφῶν
τῷ ἀδελφῷ	Dat.	τοῖς ἀδελφοῖς
τὸν ἀδελφόν	Acc.	τοὺς ἀδελφούς

<u>Note</u>: The accent changes to a circumflex in the genitive and dative cases.

The Grave Accent

An acute accent (´) on the <u>ultima</u> changes to a grave (`) when an accented word follows, as in the articles τὸν and τοὺς above. Some exceptions to this general rule will be treated later in Lesson 16 and in Lesson 31 of *A Course in Attic Greek, II*.

Proclitics

A proclitic is an unaccented word closely associated with the word which follows it; such a word, as suggested by its etymology, "leans" (κλίν-) "forward" (πρό). Both the nominative masculine singular and the nominative masculine plural of the definite article are proclitics. Examples: <u>ὁ</u> φίλος; <u>οἱ</u> ἀδελφοί.

Lesson 4

Genitive of Possession and Dative of Indirect Object

Genitive of Possession

The genitive case is frequently used in Greek to indicate possession, like apostrophe s or "of" in English (e.g. the man's child; the child of the man).

Attributive Position

The possessive genitive must be placed after the article of the noun possessed. This position is known as the attributive position, of which there are three variations. In the following examples, take note of the position of the genitive τοῦ ἀδελφοῦ relative to the article τοὺς of the noun υἱούς:

ὁ ἄνθρωπος παιδεύει τοὺς τοῦ ἀδελφοῦ υἱούς.
ὁ ἄνθρωπος παιδεύει τοὺς υἱούς τοὺς τοῦ ἀδελφοῦ.
ὁ ἄνθρωπος παιδεύει υἱούς τοὺς τοῦ ἀδελφοῦ.

The man is educating his brother's sons.

Dative of Indirect Object

The indirect object in Greek is expressed by the dative case. The indirect object of a sentence in English is typically denoted by "to" or "for," used to indicate the person or thing which is indirectly affected by the action of the verb (e.g. He gave a cold (direct object) to me (indirect object) or She had advice (direct object) for them (indirect object)). In Greek, consider the following example:

ὁ ἄνθρωπος πέμπει τῷ ἀδελφῷ τοὺς ἵππους.
The man is sending horses to his brother.

Prepositions

In Greek, objects of prepositions are placed in the genitive, dative, or accusative case according to the meaning of the preposition and the case which that preposition governs. Adjectival prepositional phrases are placed in the attributive position. Example:

οἱ ἐν τῷ οὐρανῷ θεοὶ οὐ διαφθείρουσι τοὺς φίλους.
The gods in heaven do not ruin their friends.

Vocabulary

λέγω, λέξω, ἔλεξα, _____, λέλεγμαι, ἐλέχθην *say, speak* (lexicon)

λείπω, λείψω, ἔλιπον, λέλοιπα, λέλειμμαι, ἐλείφθην *leave* (eclipse)

πέμπω, πέμψω, ἔπεμψα, πέπομφα, πέπεμμαι, ἐπέμφθην *send*

βίος, -ου, ὁ *life* (biography)

οὐρανός, -οῦ, ὁ *heaven, sky* (Uranus)

ποταμός, -οῦ, ὁ *river* (hippopotamus)

χρόνος, -ου, ὁ *time* (chronology)

ἀπό (+ genitive) *from, away from*

εἰς (+ accusative) *into, to*

ἐν (+ dative) *in, on, among*

Drill A

Decline:

1. ὁ χρόνος   2. ὁ ποταμός

Drill B

Conjugate:

1. λέγω   2. πέμπω

Drill C

Correct the mistakes in the accentuation, breathing, or other diacritical marks in the following words:

1. ὁ ἄνθρωπος   4. λεγόμεν
2. τούς χρόνους   5. τῶ λόγῳ
3. λεγεῖν   6. οἵ ἵπποι

Drill D

Translate the English word in parentheses into Greek, putting it in the case required by the preceding preposition; translate the completed phrase:

1. ἐν (sky)   3. εἰς (river)
2. ἀπὸ (death)   4. ἐν (friends)

Exercise A

Translate:

1. ὁ ἄνθρωπος πέμπει τοῖς φίλοις τὸν ἵππον.
2. ἐθέλετε παιδεύειν τοὺς υἱοὺς ἐν τοῖς φίλοις;
3. ἀπὸ τοῦ ποταμοῦ ἄγομεν τοὺς ἵππους.
4. ὁ θάνατος βλάπτει καὶ τὸν ἀνθρώπων λόγον.
5. ἐθέλεις διαφθείρειν τὸν τοῦ υἱοῦ βίον;

Exercise B

Translate:

1. Is he leaving his friend's horse in the river?
2. We do not wish to speak to our brothers.
3. Life among friends educates men.
4. The horse of the god is hastening into the sky.
5. Time brings death to men.

5. The so-called "Mask of Agamemnon," discovered at Mycenae
in 1876 by Heinrich Schliemann.

Lesson 5

Feminine and Neuter Nouns of the Second Declension

Feminine Nouns of the Second Declension

Feminine nouns of the second declension have the same endings as the masculine nouns. They are distinguished by the feminine forms of the definite article, ἡ. The article in Greek agrees with its noun in gender, number and case.

singular		plural
ἡ ὁδ-ός *(the) road*	Nominative	αἱ ὁδ-οί *(the) roads*
τῆς ὁδ-οῦ *of (the) road*	Genitive	τῶν ὁδ-ῶν *of (the) roads*
τῇ ὁδ-ῷ *to/for (the) road*	Dative	ταῖς ὁδ-οῖς *to/for (the) roads*
τὴν ὁδ-όν *(the) road*	Accusative	τὰς ὁδ-ούς *(the) roads*

Note: Like the masculine article, the feminine definite article in the nominative singular and plural forms is a proclitic. ex. you in y'all

Neuter Nouns of the Second Declension

Neuter nouns of the second declension differ from the masculine and feminine forms by taking -ov in the nominative singular and -α in the nominative and accusative plural, the quantity of which is short. Neuter second declension nouns are also distinguished by the neuter forms of the definite article, τό.

singular		plural
τὸ παιδί-ον *(the) child*	Nominative	τὰ παιδί-α *(the) children*
τοῦ παιδί-ου *of (the) child*	Genitive	τῶν παιδί-ων *of (the) children*
τῷ παιδί-ῳ *to/for (the) child*	Dative	τοῖς παιδί-οις *to/for (the) children*
τὸ παιδί-ον *(the) child*	Accusative	τὰ παιδί-α *(the) children*

Neuter Plural Subjects

Neuter plural nouns used as subjects take a <u>singular</u> verb.

τὰ παιδία <u>σπεύδει</u> εἰς τὸν ποταμόν.
The children <u>are hastening</u> to the river.

Persistent Accent (continued)

Circumflex Accent on the Penult in the Nominative Singular

singular		plural	singular		plural
ἡ νῆσος	Nom.	αἱ νῆσοι	τὸ δῶρον	Nom.	τὰ δῶρα
τῆς νήσου	Gen.	τῶν νήσων	τοῦ δώρου	Gen.	τῶν δώρων
τῇ νήσῳ	Dat.	ταῖς νήσοις	τῷ δώρῳ	Dat.	τοῖς δώροις
τὴν νῆσον	Acc.	τὰς νήσους	τὸ δῶρον	Acc.	τὰ δῶρα

<u>Note</u>: The circumflex accent changes to an acute when there is a <u>long ultima</u>.

Vocabulary

ἔχω, ἕξω (σχήσω), ἔσχον, ἔσχηκα, ____, ____ *have*

πείθω, πείσω, ἔπεισα, πέπεικα, πέπεισμαι, ἐπείσθην *persuade*

βιβλίον, -ου, τό *book* (Bible)

δῶρον, -ου, τό *gift* (Theodore)

κίνδυνος, -ου, ὁ *danger*

νῆσος, -ου, ἡ *island*
  (Peloponnese)

νόσος, -ου, ἡ *disease*

ὁδός, -οῦ, ἡ *road* (odometer)

οἶνος, -ου, ὁ *wine* (oenophile)

παιδίον, -ου, τό *(little) child*
  (pedagogue)

<u>Note</u>: The gender of nouns in all vocabulary lists will be indicated by the presence of the definite article: ὁ for masculine nouns, ἡ for feminine nouns, and τό for neuter nouns.

Drill A

Decline:

1. ὁ οἶνος   2. ἡ νόσος

Drill B

Supply the appropriate form of the definite article to agree with the noun provided; translate each word according to its case:

1. λόγων	4. ἀδελφός	7. παιδίου
2. ἵππους	5. ὁδῷ	8. δῶρα
3. νόσοι	6. νῆσον	9. βιβλίον

Drill C

Identify the correct form:

1. accusative plural:
   τά, ἡ, αἱ, τόν

2. nominative plural:
   τό, τούς, τοῖς, οἱ

3. dative plural:
   τῶν, τόν, τῇ, ταῖς

4. genitive singular:
   τήν, τῆς, τῶν, τῷ

5. accusative singular:
   τό, τῆς, τά, τοῦ

6. nominative singular:
   τῷ, ὁ, τά, τοῖς

Drill D

Select the correctly accented word in each group and determine why the others are incorrectly accented:

1. (a) κίνδυνου	(b) κινδῦνου	(c) κινδύνου
2. (a) οἶνῳ	(b) οἴνῳ	(c) οἰνῷ
3. (a) τόν λόγον	(b) τοῖς λογοῖς	(c) τὸν λόγον
4. (a) πόταμου	(b) ποταμού	(c) ποταμοῦ
5. (a) τῆς νόσου	(b) τὴς νόσου	(c) τής νόσου
6. (a) υἱού	(b) υἱοῦ	(c) υἷος

Exercise A

Translate:

1. ἐν χρόνῳ ὁ οἶνος βλάπτει καὶ διαφθείρει τοὺς ἀνθρώπους.
2. τὰ δῶρα πείθει καὶ τοὺς θεούς.

Exercise A (continued)

3. ἡ ὁδὸς ἄγει εἰς τὴν ἐν τῷ ποταμῷ νῆσον.
4. ὁ χρόνος καὶ ἡ νόσος κλέπτουσι τοὺς ἀνθρώπων βίους.
5. ἐθέλομεν πείθειν τοὺς θεοὺς λείπειν τὸν οὐρανόν.

Exercise B

Translate:

1. Danger is persuading the child to leave the island.
2. Even books speak to men.
3. Are you sending a gift to your son?
4. The man does not have friends on the island.
5. The children are stealing their brother's wine.

6. ὁ τοῦ οἴνου θεός.

Lesson 6

Future Active Indicative and Infinitive. Dative of Means

Future Active Indicative and Infinitive

In general, ς is the sign of the future tense in Greek. The future active indicative for ω-verbs uses the same endings as the present tense. The future stem consists of the second principal part of the verb, minus the final -ω. Example:

Principal parts: παιδεύω, <u>παιδεύσω</u>, ἐπαίδευσα, πεπαίδευκα, πεπαίδευμαι, ἐπαιδεύθην (*educate*)

Future stem: παιδεύσ-

singular	person	plural
παιδεύσ-ω *I will educate*	1	παιδεύσ-ο-μεν *We will educate*
παιδεύσ-εις *You will educate*	2	παιδεύσ-ε-τε *You will educate*
παιδεύσ-ει *He/She/It will educate*	3	παιδεύσ-ουσι(ν) *They will educate*

memorize

Infinitive   παιδεύσ-ειν
to be about to educate

<u>Note</u>: As in the present tense (see Lesson 2), the third person plural of the future active indicative can take a ν-movable.

Euphonic Changes in the Future Tense

When the σ of the future tense encounters certain types of consonants, known as mute stops, at the end of the verb stem, certain spelling or euphonic changes occur. Consider the chart below:

<u>Mute Stop</u>

	voiceless	voiced	aspirate		
<u>Labials</u>	π	β	φ	+ σ = ψ	
<u>Palatals</u>	κ	γ	χ	+ σ = ξ	
<u>Dentals</u>	τ	δ	θ	+ σ = σ	<u>Note</u>: Dentals <u>drop</u>.

Examples:

Labials: γράφω → γράψω
        λείπω → λείψω
        πέμπω → πέμψω

Palatals: ἄγω → ἄξω
         λέγω → λέξω

Dentals: πείθω → πείσω
        σπεύδω → σπεύσω.

<u>Note</u>: The mute stops are named according to the way they are pronounced. Labials are said using the lips, palatals the tongue on the palate or roof of the mouth, and dentals with the tongue on the teeth. Voiced mutes require vocal cord vibration; voiceless ones do not. Aspirates add a breathing or "h" sound.

Some verbs undergo more complex euphonic change because they end with a combination of mutes. The verbs below end in both a labial and a dental:

βλάπτω → βλάψω
κλέπτω → κλέψω

Verbs ending in double tau, like φυλάττω (*guard*), behave like palatals:

φυλάττω → φυλάξω

Dative of Means

The dative case, <u>without</u> a preposition, is used to express the means or instrument by which an action is performed. Example:

ὁ ἄνθρωπος τὸ παιδίον <u>δώροις</u> πείσει.
The man will persuade the child <u>with (by means of) gifts</u>.

Postpositive Words

Postpositive words never stand first in a sentence or clause. Example:

οὐκ ἐθέλω λέγειν τῷ ἀνθρώπῳ· παιδία <u>γὰρ</u> διαφθείρει.
I do not want to speak to the man; <u>for</u> he corrupts children.

Vocabulary

κελεύω, κελεύσω, ἐκέλευσα, κεκέλευκα, κεκέλευσμαι, ἐκελεύσθην
  order, command

μέλλω, μελλήσω, ἐμέλλησα, _____, _____, _____ (+ future infinitive)
  be about (to), intend (to), be likely (to), be going (to)

φυλάττω, φυλάξω, ἐφύλαξα, πεφύλαχα, πεφύλαγμαι, ἐφυλάχθην
  guard

λίθος, -ου, ὁ *stone* (lithography)   ἀλλά *but*

πλοῦτος, -ου, ὁ *wealth*   γάρ (postpositive word) *for*
       (plutocracy)
                                                       δέ (postpositive word) *and; but*
πόλεμος, -ου, ὁ *war* (polemic)

στρατηγός, -οῦ, ὁ *general*
       (strategy)

Drill A

Predict the second principal part of the following unfamiliar Greek verbs:

1.	τρέπω	4.	ἥκω
2.	πιστεύω	5.	θύω
3.	ἄρχω	6.	θάπτω

Drill B

Parse and translate the following forms:

1.	κελεύσομεν	6.	ἔχομεν
2.	φυλάξειν	7.	διαφθείρειν
3.	μέλλουσι	8.	λέξεις
4.	γράψετε	9.	μελλήσω
5.	πείσειν	10.	βλάψουσι

Drill C

Change the verb from the present to the future or vice versa; translate the result:

1. φυλάξει   4. πείθουσι
2. λείψετε   5. λέξομεν
3. ἔχω   6. ἄξεις

Drill D

Translate:

1. You (pl.) will steal   4. We harm
2. I will persuade   5. To intend (to)
3. To be about to hasten   6. They will order

Exercise A

Translate:

1. ἐν χρόνῳ οἱ ἐν τῷ οὐρανῷ θεοὶ ἄξουσι τοῖς ἀνθρώποις τὸν θάνατον.
2. τῷ πλούτῳ οἱ θεοὶ τοὺς ἀνθρώπους διαφθείρουσι.
3. οὐ πέμψομεν τὸν οἶνον· ὁ γὰρ οἶνος παιδία βλάπτει.
4. ἐθέλει πλοῦτον ἔχειν, τὰ δὲ δῶρα οὐ κλέψει.
5. ὁ τοῦ πολέμου κίνδυνος πείσει τοὺς στρατηγοὺς λείπειν τοὺς υἱοὺς ἐν τῇ νήσῳ.

Exercise B

Translate:

1. With reason and gifts he intends to persuade the general to guard his children.
2. Are you (pl.) going to send the books to your friends?
3. War harms the lives of men; for it is likely to bring disease and death.
4. I will order my brother to guard the road, but he will not be willing.
5. Will you (sg.) hurt the children with stones?

Lesson 7

Feminine Nouns of the First Declension (Category I). Balanced Structure

<u>Category I Feminine Nouns of the First Declension</u>

This chapter will introduce Category I nouns of the first declension. Categories II and III will be introduced later in Lesson 18.

Category I first declension nouns, like the vast majority of first declension nouns in Greek, are <u>feminine</u> in gender. Category Ia first declension nouns end in -η in the nominative singular; their stem is found by dropping -ης from the genitive singular. Category Ib first declension nouns end in -ᾱ in the nominative singular; they are distinguished by having a <u>stem</u> – found by dropping -ας from the genitive singular – that ends in ε, ι or ρ (e.g. οἰκία or ἀγορά). This stem causes category Ib first declension nouns to feature α rather than η in their singular declensional endings.

<u>Feminine First Declension Nouns (Category Ia, -η)</u>

<u>singular</u>		<u>plural</u>
ἡ ἀρετ-ή *(the) virtue*	Nominative	αἱ ἀρετ-αί *(the) virtues*
τῆς ἀρετ-ῆς *of (the) virtue*	Genitive	τῶν ἀρετ-ῶν *of (the) virtues*
τῇ ἀρετ-ῇ *to/for (the) virtue*	Dative	ταῖς ἀρετ-αῖς *to/for (the) virtues*
τὴν ἀρετ-ήν *(the) virtue*	Accusative	τὰς ἀρετ-άς *(the) virtues*

<u>Feminine First Declension Nouns (Category Ib, -ᾱ)</u>

<u>singular</u>		<u>plural</u>
ἡ οἰκί-α *(the) house*	Nominative	αἱ οἰκί-αι *(the) houses*
τῆς οἰκί-ας *of (the) house*	Genitive	τῶν οἰκι-ῶν *of (the) houses*
τῇ οἰκί-ᾳ *to/for (the) house*	Dative	ταῖς οἰκί-αις *to/for (the) houses*
τὴν οἰκί-αν *(the) house*	Accusative	τὰς οἰκί-ας *(the) houses*

Exercise A

Translate:

1. ἐθέλετε παρέχειν τὰ δῶρα τοῖς ἀδελφοῖς;
2. τὰ παιδία σπεύσει ἀπὸ τῶν οἰκιῶν εἰς τὴν ἀγοράν.
3. λόγῳ μὲν οὐ πείσει τὴν στρατιὰν λείπειν τὴν ἀγοράν, πλούτῳ δέ.
4. οἱ μὲν τοῖς λόγοις καὶ ταῖς γνώμαις παιδεύουσι τὰ παιδία, οἱ δὲ τῇ ἀρετῇ.
5. τὰ δῶρα τοῖς θεοῖς πέμψομεν, ἐθέλομεν γὰρ εἰρήνην ἄγειν.

Exercise B

Translate:

1. Some trust the judgment of the general, others trust the justice of the gods.
2. Wealth provides slander among men, but reason provides justice.
3. Peace brings wealth, but war brings the danger of disease and death.
4. The general will lead his army from the road to the river.
5. Wealth and slander harm justice; the one men wish to have, the other they wish to speak.

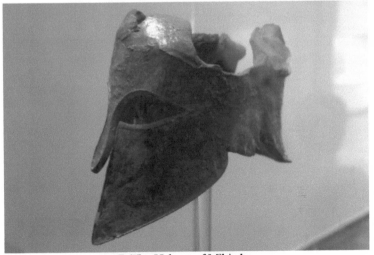

7. The Helmet of Miltiades,
general at The Battle of Marathon, 489 BC.

Lesson 8

First and Second Aorist Active Indicative and Infinitive
Verbal Aspect

The Aorist Tense. Verbal Aspect

The aorist is a past tense that expresses a single action of no significant duration. The perspective from which an action is described is called its aspect. The aorist has a simple aspect: *I educated.* It is like a digital snapshot of a past action. Simple aspect contrasts with progressive aspect, which focuses on the unfolding of an action or whether it is repeated or habitual. If the aorist is like a digital snapshot, a tense with a progressive aspect, like the imperfect (see Lesson 13; *I was educating, I kept on educating*, or *I used to educate*) is like a video replay of an action.

Temporal Augment

The aorist tense only has time value in the indicative mood. In all other verbal moods, it expresses aspect only. As such, the aorist only takes a temporal augment in the indicative mood. The augment is a spelling change at the beginning of the aorist stem. This augment is always included as part of the third principal part of the verb, but it can usually be predicted from the verb's first principal part as follows:

1) If the first principal part begins with a <u>consonant</u>, ἐ is prefixed to the stem. Example:
   παιδεύω → ἐπαίδευσα

2) If the verb begins with a <u>vowel</u>, that vowel is typically lengthened as follows:

   (a) α or ε → η (<u>Note</u>: αυ or ευ → ηυ)
       ἀδικέω → ἠδίκησα
       ἐθέλω → ἠθέλησα

   (b) ο → ω
       ὁμολογέω → ὡμολόγησα

   (c) η or ω → no change
       ὠφελέω → ὠφέλησα

   (d) ι or υ → no <u>visible</u> change, however, the quantity or the vowel becomes long

   (e) any vowel + ι → augmented vowel with iota subscript (<u>Note</u>: if the subscript is already present in the first principal part, it remains as part of the augment)
       αἰτέω → ᾔτησα
       οἰκέω → ᾤκησα

The First Aorist Active Indicative and Infinitive

The aorist tense is made up of the first and second aorist conjugations. While first and second aorists are formed differently, they typically do not differ in meaning. The first aorist conjugation is far more common than the second aorist conjugation. A verb is a first aorist if it has a third principal part that ends in -σα, or a variant of -σα, like -ψα or -ξα. The first aorist active stem is found by dropping the -σα from the third principal part of the verb and adding the endings below. The first aorist does not employ a thematic vowel between the stem and ending:

singular	person	plural
ἐ-παίδευ-σα *I educated*	1	ἐ-παιδεύ-σα-μεν *We educated*
ἐ-παίδευ-σα-ς	2	ἐ-παιδεύ-σα-τε
You educated		*You educated*
ἐ-παίδευ-σε(ν)	3	ἐ-παίδευ-σα-ν
He / She /It educated		*They educated*

Infinitive παιδεῦ-σαι
to educate

Notes: A ν-movable is added to the end of all verbs in Greek that end in an -ε in the third person singular, as ἐπαίδευσε above.

The aorist infinitive only has time value in indirect statement (see *A Course in Attic Greek* II, Lesson 32). As such, it does not receive a temporal augment, since it primarily expresses aspect. In contrast to the present infinitive, "to be educating," which has a progressive aspect and focuses on the unfolding of an action (like a video), the aorist infinitive, "to educate," has a simple aspect and focuses on the simple occurrence of the action (like a snapshot).

The first aorist active infinitive is <u>always</u> accented on the <u>penult</u>. The final -σαι of the first aorist active infinitive is considered short for purposes of accentuation. Examples:

παιδεῦσαι   ἐθελῆσαι   γράψαι

The Second Aorist Active Indicative and Infinitive

A second aorist has a third principal part that ends in -ον. The aorist active stem of a second aorist is found by dropping the -ον from the end of the third principal part and adding the endings as below. The stem of a second aorist is typically spelled differently than the first principal part, often featuring reduplication (e.g. ἄγω → ἤγαγον) or a degradation of the verb's vowel sound (e.g. λείπω → ἔλιπον). The second aorist of some verbs, however, is somewhat unpredictable (e.g. ἔχω → ἔσχον) and so must be memorized. Unlike the first aorist, the second aorist <u>does employ</u> a thematic vowel between stem and personal ending, separated in the chart, where possible, by a dash:

singular	person	plural
ἔ-λιπ-ο-ν	1	ἐ-λίπ-ο-μεν
I left		*We left*
ἔ-λιπ-ε-ς	2	ἐ-λίπ-ε-τε
You left		*You left*
ἔ-λιπ-ε(ν)	3	ἔ-λιπ-ον
He / She / It left		*They left*

Infinitive   λιπ-εῖν
to leave

<u>Note</u>: The second aorist active infinitive is formed by adding -εῖν to the stem, minus the temporal augment. This infinitive is <u>always</u> accented with a circumflex on the <u>ultima</u>. Examples:

ἀγαγεῖν (from ἄγω)   σχεῖν (from ἔχω)

Vocabulary

λύω, λύσω, ἔλυσα, λέλυκα, λέλυμαι, ἐλύθην *destroy, release, set free*
   (analysis)

παύω, παύσω, ἔπαυσα, πέπαυκα, πέπαυμαι, ἐπαύθην *stop* (pause)

σώζω, σώσω, ἔσωσα, σέσωκα, σέσωσμαι, ἐσώθην *save, bring safely*
   (creosote)

ἥλιος, -ου, ὁ *sun* (heliocentric)   ψυχή, -ῆς, ἡ *soul* (psychology)

τιμή, -ῆς, ἡ *honor* (timocracy)   διά (+ genitive) *through* (diagram)
                                                        (+ accusative) *on account of,*
χρυσίον, -ου, τό *gold*   *because of*
   (chrysanthemum)
                                                   μετά (+ genitive) *with* (metaphor)
χώρα, -ας, ἡ *country, land*   (+ accusative) *after*

Drill A

Conjugate in the aorist active indicative:

   1. ἄγω   2. σώζω   3. ἔχω

Drill B

Parse and translate the following verbs:

1. ἀγαγεῖν
2. ἐφύλαξαν
3. ἠθέλησε
4. ἕξουσι
5. μέλλεις
6. ἐθελήσει
7. ἔσχομεν
8. σχεῖν
9. λέγετε
10. πεῖσαι

Drill C

Put the verbs in the forms requested and translate:

1. λύω (aorist active indicative, third person singular)
2. λείπω (future active infinitive)
3. ἔχω (aorist active indicative, third person plural)
4. λέγω (present active indicative, second person singular)
5. παύω (future active indicative, first person singular)
6. φυλάττω (aorist active infinitive)
7. σώζω (present active indicative, first person plural)
8. ἐθέλω (aorist active indicative, second person plural)

Drill D

Put the noun in parentheses in the case indicated or that which is required by the preceding preposition; translate the completed phrase:

1. οἱ ἵπποι διὰ (ἡ χώρα, genitive singular) ἔσπευσαν.
2. οἱ θεοὶ ἀπὸ (ὁ θάνατος, singular) τὴν ψυχὴν σώσουσιν.
3. τὰ παιδία εἰς (ἡ οἰκία, singular) ἐπέμψαμεν.
4. οἱ ἄνθρωποι μετὰ (ὁ φίλος, genitive plural) ἔλιπον.
5. ὁ στρατηγὸς διὰ (ἡ ἀρετή, accusative singular) τὴν τιμὴν ἔχει.
6. μετὰ (ὁ πόλεμος, accusative singular), ἡ στρατιὰ τὴν εἰρήνην
   ἐν (ἡ χώρα, singular) παρέσχε.

Exercise A

Translate:

1. οἱ μὲν χρυσίῳ τοὺς ἀνθρώπους πείσουσι λῦσαι τὴν τιμήν, οἱ δὲ λόγοις.

2. τὰ τοῦ στρατηγοῦ παιδία ἔσπευσε διὰ τῆς χώρας μετὰ τῶν φίλων.

3. διὰ τὴν διαβολὴν οὐκ ἐπιστεύσαμεν τοῖς ἀδελφοῖς.

4. ἡ τῶν θεῶν δίκη τὸν πόλεμον ἔπαυσε, καὶ τὴν στρατιὰν ἔσωσε.

5. μετὰ τὸν πόλεμον ἡ στρατιὰ ἐφύλαξε τὰς ἐν τῇ νήσῳ οἰκίας.

Exercise B

Translate:

1. After death the gods will bring the souls of men safely into heaven.

2. The sun provides life for men.

3. Did you (sg.) persuade your son to steal the gold?

4. War corrupts and destroys the souls of men.

5. The general did not lead his army, for he wished to stop the war on account of the danger of disease and death.

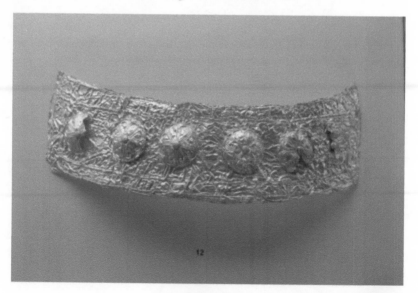

8. τὸ χρυσίον.

Lesson 9

Adjectives of the First and Second Declensions. Irregular Adjectives

Adjectives of the First and Second Declensions

In Greek, an adjective is declined to agree with the noun it modifies in gender, number, and case. Adjectives of the first and second declensions are classified into two groups as follows:

Adjectives of three terminations.

πρῶτος, πρώτη, πρῶτον *first*

singular

	masculine	feminine	neuter
Nom.	πρῶτ-ος	πρώτ-η	πρῶτ-ον
Gen.	πρώτ-ου	πρώτ-ης	πρώτ-ου
Dat.	πρώτ-ῳ	πρώτ-ῃ	πρώτ-ῳ
Acc.	πρῶτ-ον	πρώτ-ην	πρῶτ-ον

plural

Nom.	πρῶτ-οι	πρῶτ-αι	πρῶτ-α
Gen.	πρώτ-ων	πρώτ-ων	πρώτ-ων
Dat.	πρώτ-οις	πρώτ-αις	πρώτ-οις
Acc.	πρώτ-ους	πρώτ-ας	πρῶτ-α

Note: Like nouns of the first declension, adjectives with a feminine stem ending in ε, ι or ρ have -α instead of -η in the feminine forms. Example: δίκαιος, δικαία, δίκαιον.

Unlike nouns of the first declension, which always have a circumflex on the ultima of the genitive plural, adjectives in the feminine genitive plural follow the normal rules for accentuation.

Adjectives of two terminations. These adjectives have one set of endings for the masculine and feminine gender and another set for the neuter gender. Most two termination adjectives feature the negative prefix (α-), known as "alpha privative," because the α- "deprives" the adjective of its original meaning. We use an alpha privative in such English words as "amoral" and "amorphous." Not all adjectives in Greek, however, that begin with an α- feature an alpha privative, only those where the α- negates the original meaning of the adjective. Examples:

Normal α: ἄξιος,-α,-ον *worthy (of)*
Alpha privative: ἄδικος, ἄδικον *unjust*

singular

	masculine-feminine	neuter
Nom.	ἄδικ-ος	ἄδικ-ον
Gen.	ἀδίκ-ου	ἀδίκ-ου
Dat.	ἀδίκ-ῳ	ἀδίκ-ῳ
Acc.	ἄδικ-ον	ἄδικ-ον

plural

	masculine-feminine	neuter
Nom.	ἄδικ-οι	ἄδικ-α
Gen.	ἀδίκ-ων	ἀδίκ-ων
Dat.	ἀδίκ-οις	ἀδίκ-οις
Acc.	ἀδίκ-ους	ἄδικ-α

Irregular Adjectives. The following adjectives show irregularities, which are underlined, in the nominative and accusative singular in the masculine and neuter genders:

μέγας, μεγάλη, μέγα *large, great*

singular

	masculine	feminine	neuter
Nom.	μέγας	μεγάλ-η	μέγα
Gen.	μεγάλ-ου	μεγάλ-ης	μεγάλ-ου
Dat.	μεγάλ-ῳ	μεγάλ-ῃ	μεγάλ-ῳ
Acc.	μέγαν	μεγάλ-ην	μέγα

plural

	masculine	feminine	neuter
Nom.	μεγάλ-οι	μεγάλ-αι	μεγάλ-α
Gen.	μεγάλ-ων	μεγάλ-ων	μεγάλ-ων
Dat.	μεγάλ-οις	μεγάλ-αις	μεγάλ-οις
Acc.	μεγάλ-ους	μεγάλ-ας	μεγάλ-α

Drill B

Give the following forms and translate the adjective-noun pair:

1. ἀθάνατος to agree with: ψυχῇ, βίου, τιμῶν, δῶρα
2. δεινός to agree with: στρατηγῶν, φίλοι, νόσῳ, δίκην
3. ἄξιος to agree with: ὁδούς, ἀρετῇ, γνωμῶν, παιδία
4. πολύς to agree with: χρυσίον, οἶνον, νῆσοι, χρόνου

Drill C

Supply the appropriate form of the adjective to agree with the noun provided; indicate whether the adjective is in attributive or predicate position and translate accordingly:

1. τῶν (just) ἀνθρώπων
2. τῆς (first) νήσου
3. τὰ δῶρα (fine)
4. τῇ (great) ἀρετῇ
5. ὁ ἥλιος (large)
6. τοῖς θανάτοις τοῖς (terrible)
7. ἡ γνώμη (wise)
8. (unjust) ἡ τιμή

Drill D

Supply the appropriate form of the substantive adjective; translate the completed sentence:

1. ὁ στρατηγὸς τοὺς πολλοὺς πολέμους καὶ (evil things) εἰς τὴν χώραν ἤγαγε.
2. τὰς (unjust men, genitive) διαβολὰς παύσειν ἐμελλήσαμεν.
3. (Wise men, nominative) τὰ παιδία παιδεύσουσιν.

Exercise A

Translate:

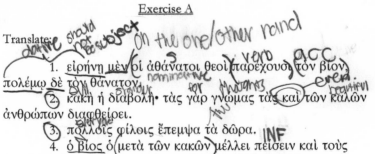

1. εἰρήνη μὲν οἱ ἀθάνατοι θεοὶ παρέχουσι τὸν βίον, πολέμῳ δὲ τὸν θάνατον.
2. κακὴ ἡ διαβολή· τὰς γὰρ γνώμας τὰς καὶ τῶν καλῶν ἀνθρώπων διαφθείρει.
3. πολλοῖς φίλοις ἔπεμψα τὰ δῶρα.
4. ὁ βίος ὁ μετὰ τῶν κακῶν μέλλει πείσειν καὶ τοὺς δικαίους κλέπτειν τὸ χρυσίον καὶ λέγειν ἀδίκους λόγους.
5. πιστεύω τοῖς τοῦ ἀδελφοῦ φίλοις τοῖς καλοῖς.

Exercise B

Translate:

     1. The fine general is worthy of honor, for he brought many children safely through the country.

     2. The souls of men are immortal.

     3. Unjust words are not likely to harm just men.

     4. After the great war, terrible diseases destroyed the lives of many wise generals.

     5. The clever child is about to speak his first words.

9. The Caryatids, supporting the south roof of
The Erechtheion (406 BC) on the Acropolis, Athens.

Lesson 10

Review

Drill A

Translate:

1. διαφθείρομεν	6. οὐ πιστεύσει
2. ἔπαυσα	7. ἔλιπες
3. οὐκ ἄξει	8. σώσω
4. ἔσχετε	9. ἐφύλαξαν
5. μελλήσεις λέξειν	10. παρέξετε

Drill B

Translate:

1. they led	6. I left
2. you (pl.) will harm	7. they will not have
3. he is writing	8. I persuaded
4. we hastened	9. we are educating
5. you (sg.) do order	10. he does not wish to steal

Drill C

Give the following forms in Greek and translate:

1. genitive plural of:
   ἡ πρώτη οἰκία, πόλεμος, ποταμός, τὸ δῶρον τὸ καλόν

2. dative singular of:
   ἡ ἄδικος γνώμη, ἡ μεγάλη χώρα, ἡ δεινὴ νόσος,
   ὁ πρῶτος λίθος

3. accusative plural of:
   the bad children, many roads, the large islands,
   the immortal gods

Exercise A

Translate:

1. ὁ κακὸς ἄξιος θανάτου· τοὺς γὰρ φίλους διαφθείρει οἴνῳ καὶ κακαῖς γνώμαις.
2. διὰ πολλὰ οὐκ ἔκλεψε τοὺς τοῦ στρατηγοῦ ἵππους.
3. οἱ μὲν λόγοις καὶ βιβλίοις παιδεύουσι τὰ παιδία, οἱ δὲ δικαίαις γνώμαις καὶ ἀρετῇ.
4. τὸ παιδίον δεινὸν λέγειν, ἀλλὰ τοὺς ἀδελφοὺς οὐ πείσει.
5. πολλοὶ ἔχουσι πολὺν πλοῦτον.

Exercise B

Translate:

1. Did you (pl.) trust the words of your unjust friends in the market-place?
2. The immortal gods in heaven are great, for they send peace and justice and stop wars.
3. With a large stone he persuaded the children to hasten from his beautiful island.
4. The great general educated many friends worthy of note ("worthy of note" = ἄξιος, -α, -ον λόγου).
5. Some had wealth and honor, but others had prejudice and evil thoughts.

10. Bronze ballots (ψῆφοι) for use in the lawcourts of Athens, fourth century BC.

Lesson 11

Present Middle-Passive Indicative and Infinitive
Future Middle Indicative and Infinitive
Deponent and Semi-deponent Verbs. Genitive of Personal Agent

The Passive Voice

While the active voice signifies that a subject does the action of the verb (e.g. the boy (subject) throws (active verb) the ball (direct object)), the passive voice signifies that a subject receives the action of the verb (e.g. the ball (subject) is thrown (passive verb)) and is acted upon by someone or something <u>other than itself</u>.

The Middle Voice

The middle voice is something of a hybrid voice. In the middle voice, the subject both does an action and receives some kind of playback from it, that is to say, the subject either acts <u>upon itself</u> or <u>in its own interest</u> in some way. Some basic uses of the middle voice follow:

The boy <u>throws himself</u>
Here the subject, the boy, acts directly upon himself rather than upon a direct object.

The boy <u>throws</u> a ball <u>for himself</u>
Here the subject, the boys, acts in his own interest by throwing the ball for himself rather than for another person.

The middle voice is also used in Greek to express intransitive ideas, where the subject, as in the first example, acts upon itself rather than on a direct object. Examples:

I stand up the statue (transitive verb)
I stand (up) (intransitive verb)

παύω τὸν ἄνθρωπον.   *I stop the man* (transitive verb)
παύομαι   *I stop myself*, i.e. *I cease* (intransitive verb)

The idea of self-interest as expressed by the middle voice in Greek can be extended quite broadly. Examples:

The Athenians <u>pass</u> a law

Here the verb "pass" would be expressed in the middle voice in Greek since the Athenians "pass the law" as a means to govern <u>themselves</u>.

I <u>educate</u> my son
Here, the verb "educate" would be expressed in the middle voice in Greek, since it is in the interest of a father that his own son be educated.

Finally, some verbs in Greek take special idiomatic meanings in the middle voice. Examples:

πείθομαι (+ dative case) *I persuade myself*, hence *I obey*

βουλεύομαι *I plan for myself*, hence *I deliberate*

Present Middle-Passive Indicative and Infinitive

In the present, perfect, and pluperfect tenses, the forms of the middle and passive voice are indistinguishable from one another. As such, a form like παιδεύομαι is ambiguous is meaning; it may be either middle or passive. As a middle form, it may be translated *I educate myself / for my benefit*. As a passive form, it may be translated as *I am educated*. Context will determine the best translation, of which more will be said below.

The present middle-passive indicative for ω-verbs is formed by adding an ending to the present stem (i.e. the first principal part minus -ω). Like the active voice, the ending is made up of a thematic vowel and a personal ending, separated in the chart below where possible with a dash. Primary tense verbs (i.e. the present, future, and perfect tense verbs) all use the same middle-passive personal endings. Secondary tense verbs (i.e. the imperfect, aorist, and pluperfect), all of which are augmented, use a different set of middle-passive endings (see Lesson 12).

singular	person	plural
παιδεύ-ο-μαι	1	παιδευ-ό-μεθα
I educate (for) myself (mid.)		*We educate (for) ourselves* (mid.)
I am educated (pass.)		*We are educated* (pass.)
παιδεύ-ει (-η)	2	παιδεύ-ε-σθε
You educate (for) yourself (mid.)		*You educate (for) yourselves* (mid.)
You are educated (pass.)		*You are educated* (pass.)
παιδεύ-ε-ται	3	παιδεύ-ο-νται
He/She/It educates (for)		*They educate (for)*
him-/her-/itself (mid.)		*themselves* (mid.)
He/She/It is educated (pass.)		*They are educated* (pass.)

Infinitive   παιδεύ-ε-σθαι
to be educating oneself (mid.)
to be educated (pass.)

Notes: The second person singular form (παιδεύ-ε-σαι) is the result of a contraction. The uncontracted form would be παιδεύ-ε-σαι. In Greek, intervocalic sigma (i.e. a sigma falling between two vowels) is often unstable. In this particular form, intervocalic sigma drops and the remaining vowel sounds combine as follows:

$$\pi\alpha\iota\delta\epsilon\acute{u}\epsilon[\sigma]\alpha\iota \rightarrow \pi\alpha\iota\delta\epsilon\acute{u}\epsilon\alpha\iota \rightarrow \pi\alpha\iota\delta\epsilon\acute{u}\epsilon\iota \text{ or } \pi\alpha\iota\delta\epsilon\acute{u}\eta$$

The more common contracted form, παιδεύει, presents the additional difficulty of looking identical to the present active indicative, third person singular form. Thus, παιδεύει may be translated as follows: *he educates* (third person singular active); *you educate (for) yourself* (second person singular middle); or *you are educated* (second person singular passive). Context will determine the appropriate translation.

Future Middle Indicative and Infinitive

Unlike the present tense, the future tense has separate forms for the middle and passive voices. The future middle indicative for ω-verbs is formed by adding the primary middle passive endings – those used for the present middle-passive – to the future active stem (i.e. the second principal part minus -ω).

singular	person	plural
παιδεύσο-ο-μαι *I will educate (for) myself*	1	παιδευσο-ό-μεθα *We will educate (for) ourselves*
παιδεύσο-ει (-η) *You will educate (for) yourself*	2	παιδεύσο-ε-σθε *You will educate (for) yourselves*
παιδεύσο-ε-ται *He/She/It will educate (for) him-/her-/itself*	3	παιδεύσο-ο-νται *They will educate (for) themselves*

Infinitive παιδεύσο-ε-σθαι
to be about to educate (for) oneself

Notes: As in the present tense, the second person singular form (παιδεύσει (-η)) is the result of a contraction, caused by the loss of intervocalic sigma as follows:

$$\pi\alpha\iota\delta\epsilon\acute{u}\sigma\epsilon[\sigma]\alpha\iota \rightarrow \pi\alpha\iota\delta\epsilon\acute{u}\sigma\epsilon\alpha\iota \rightarrow \pi\alpha\iota\delta\epsilon\acute{u}\sigma\epsilon\iota \text{ or } \pi\alpha\iota\delta\epsilon\acute{u}\sigma\eta$$

As in the present tense, παιδεύσει is an ambiguous form, translated as *he will educate* (third person singular active) or *you will educate (for) yourself* (second person singular middle).

Deponent and Semi-deponent Verbs

Deponent verbs are a class of verbs that have middle and passive forms only, but are translated actively. Example:

ἀφικνέομαι, ἀφίξομαι, ἀφικόμην, _____, ἀφῖγμαι _____ *arrive (in),*
arrive (at), reach

Often deponent verbs are intransitive, as ἀφικνέομαι above, or specify an action in which the subject both acts and is affected in someway by its action. In the case of the deponent verb βούλομαι, for example, which means "to want," the subject performs the action of "wanting," but also receives some kind of playback from it, namely he satisfies a desire that will have some kind of effect on him.

Semi-deponent verbs have middle and passive forms only in certain tenses, particularly in the future. Example:

φεύγω, <u>φεύξομαι,</u> ἔφυγον, πέφευγα, _____, _____ *flee, escape, avoid*

Genitive of Personal Agent

The genitive with the preposition ὑπὸ is used in Greek to indicate the person (or <u>agent</u>) by whom the action of a passive verb is performed. Example:

<u>ὑπὸ τοῦ στρατηγοῦ</u> πέμπεται.
He is being sent <u>by the general</u>.

The presence of a genitive of personal agent can help to resolve the ambiguity of a verb form that may be either middle or passive in voice: if a genitive of agent is present, assume that the verb is in the passive voice.

Vocabulary

ἀκούω, ἀκούσομαι, ἤκουσα, ἀκήκοα, _____, ἠκούσθην (+ genitive) *hear,*
listen to (acoustic) Semi deponent

ἄρχω, ἄρξω, ἦρξα, ἦρχα, ἦργμαι, ἤρχθην (+ genitive) *rule;* (in *takes genitive object*
the middle voice) *begin* (monarch) regular

βουλεύω, βουλεύσω, ἐβούλευσα, βεβούλευκα, βεβούλευμαι,
ἐβουλεύθην *plan;* (in the middle voice) *deliberate* Semi

ἔρχομαι, ἐλεύσομαι, ἦλθον, ἐλήλυθα, _____, _____ *come; go*

λαμβάνω, λήψομαι, ἔλαβον, εἴληφα, εἴλημμαι, ἐλήφθην *take, seize;*
receive (prolepsis) Semi deponent

πάσχω, πείσομαι, ἔπαθον, πέπονθα, _____, _____ *suffer* (pathetic)

φεύγω, φεύξομαι, ἔφυγον, πέφευγα, _____, _____ *flee, escape, avoid*
(fugitive)

νέος, -α, -ον *young; new; strange*   ὑπό (+ genitive) *by, at the hands of,*
(neophyte)   *under*
                                                                     (+ accusative) *under* (with verbs
                                                                     of motion) (hypodermic)

Note: The future middle forms of πάσχω and πείθω look <u>identical</u>.

Drill A

Conjugate:

    1. future middle of ἄρχω
    2. aorist active of ἔρχομαι
    3. present middle-passive of ἀκούω

Drill B

Parse and translate:

    1. πείθεσθαι   6. λήψεται
    2. φεύξεσθε   7. λυόμεθα
    3. ἀκούσει   8. ἤκουσαν
    4. ἐλθεῖν   9. βουλεύσονται
    5. ἐλάβομεν   10. βουλεῦσαι

Drill C

Change the form of the verb to the voice indicated in parentheses;
translate the result:

    1. βλάπτεις (passive)   6. ἄρξομεν (middle)
    2. πάσχονται (active)   7. λαμβάνεται (active)
    3. ἄξουσι (middle)   8. βουλεύσω (middle)
    4. παύει, third person (passive)   9. σώσεσθε (active)
    5. λύσεις (middle)   10. πιστεύομαι (active)

Drill D

Translate:

1. We will come
2. I begin
3. They will suffer

4. He will hear
5 You (pl.) obey
6. You (sg.) listened

Exercise A

Translate:

1. τοὺς νέους παιδευσόμεθα ἐν τῇ ἀγορᾷ.
2. τὰ καλὰ δῶρα τοῖς παιδίοις ὑπὸ τῶν φίλων
πέμπεται.
3. οἱ μὲν τὸν κίνδυνον φεύξονται καὶ τοὺς βίους
σώσονται· οἱ δὲ τὸν θάνατον πείσονται ἐν τῷ πολέμῳ.
4. ἔρχει εἰς τὴν χώραν τὴν τῶν δικαίων καὶ τῶν σοφῶν;
5. διὰ τῆς καλῆς χώρας ἦλθον μετὰ μεγάλης στρατιᾶς,
ἀλλὰ τοῦ πολέμου οὐκ ἐμέλλησαν ἄρξεσθαι.

Exercise B

Translate:

1. Do you wish to hear the clever men and be educated?
2. The unjust do not obey the immortal gods.
3. I went to my brother's house and received much wine.
4. He will not deliberate, but he will say many things.
5. The lives of men are ruled by the immortal gods in heaven.

Lesson 12

Demonstratives
First and Second Aorist Middle Indicative and Infinitive

Demonstratives

The demonstratives ἐκεῖνος ("that"), οὗτος ("this"), and ὅδε ("this") are declined as follows:

<u>singular</u>

	<u>masculine</u>	<u>feminine</u>	<u>neuter</u>
Nom.	ἐκεῖνος	ἐκείνη	<u>ἐκεῖνο</u>
Gen.	ἐκείνου	ἐκείνης	ἐκείνου
Dat.	ἐκείνῳ	ἐκείνῃ	ἐκείνῳ
Acc.	ἐκεῖνον	ἐκείνην	<u>ἐκεῖνο</u>

<u>plural</u>

	masculine	feminine	neuter
Nom.	ἐκεῖνοι	ἐκεῖναι	ἐκεῖνα
Gen.	ἐκείνων	ἐκείνων	ἐκείνων
Dat.	ἐκείνοις	ἐκείναις	ἐκείνοις
Acc.	ἐκείνους	ἐκείνας	ἐκεῖνα

<u>Note</u>: The demonstrative ἐκεῖνος is declined similarly to an adjective of the first and second declensions (see Lesson 9), with the exception of the nominative and accusative neuter singular, underlined above, which end in -ο rather than -ον.

<u>singular</u>

	<u>masculine</u>	<u>feminine</u>	<u>neuter</u>
Nom.	<u>οὗτος</u>	<u>αὕτη</u>	<u>τοῦτο</u>
Gen.	τούτου	ταύτης	τούτου
Dat.	τούτῳ	ταύτῃ	τούτῳ
Acc.	τοῦτον	ταύτην	<u>τοῦτο</u>

<u>plural</u>

Nom.	οὗτοι	αὗται	ταῦτα
Gen.	τούτων	τούτων	τούτων
Dat.	τούτοις	ταύταις	τούτοις
Acc.	τούτους	ταύτας	ταῦτα

<u>singular</u>

	<u>masculine</u>	<u>feminine</u>	<u>neuter</u>
Nom.	ὅδε	ἥδε	τόδε
Gen.	τοῦδε	τῆσδε	τοῦδε
Dat.	τῷδε	τῇδε	τῷδε
Acc.	τόνδε	τήνδε	τόδε

<u>plural</u>

Nom.	οἵδε	αἵδε	τάδε
Gen.	τῶνδε	τῶνδε	τῶνδε
Dat.	τοῖσδε	ταῖσδε	τοῖσδε
Acc.	τούσδε	τάσδε	τάδε

<u>Note</u>: The forms of ὅδε are essentially a combination of forms of the definite article plus the suffix -δε.

Uses of the Demonstratives

a. When demonstratives are used as adjectives, they are placed in the <u>predicate</u> position. Examples:

<u>ἐκεῖνος</u> ὁ κίνδυνος   <u>that</u> danger
<u>αὕτη</u> ἡ νῆσος   <u>this</u> island
τὸ βιβλίον <u>τόδε</u>   <u>this</u> book

b. Like adjectives, demonstratives may also be used substantively. As substantives, demonstratives are often best translated as third person personal pronouns. Examples:

<u>ἐκείνων</u> ἠκούσατε.
You heard <u>those ones</u>/ <u>men</u>/ <u>women</u>/ <u>things</u>. or You heard <u>them</u>.

τούτῳ οὐ πείθομαι.
I do not obey this man. or *I do not obey him.*

ταῦτα ἔλεξε.
He said these things. or *He said this.*

οὗτοι μὲν τὸν θάνατον πείσονται, ἐκεῖνοι δὲ φεύξονται.
These (men) (on one hand) will suffer death, (but) those (men) (on the other hand) will flee.

ἐκλέψαμεν τὸ ἐκείνων χρυσίον.
We stole the gold of those ones/men/women. or *We stole their gold.*

First Aorist Middle Indicative and Infinitive

Like the future tense, the aorist tense has separate forms of the verb for the middle and passive voices. The stem for the first aorist middle is the third principal part in its entirety. To this stem, the secondary middle-passive endings are added, without the use of a thematic vowel:

singular	person	plural
ἐ-παιδεύ-σα-μην	1	ἐ-παιδευ-σά-μεθα
I educated (for) myself		*We educated (for) ourselves*
ἐ-παιδεύ-σω	2	ἐ-παιδεύ-σα-σθε
You educated (for) yourself		*You educated (for) yourselves*
ἐ-παιδεύ-σα-το	3	ἐ-παιδεύ-σα-ντο
He/She/It educated (for) him-/her-/itself		*They educated (for) themselves*

Infinitive παιδεύ-σα-σθαι
to educate (for) oneself

Notes: As in the present middle-passive and future middle, the second person singular form (ἐπαιδεύσω), is the result of a contraction, caused by the loss of intervocalic sigma as follows.

ἐπαιδεύσα[σ]ο → ἐπαιδεύσαο → ἐπαιδεύσω

As in the aorist active infinitive, the aorist middle infinitive receives no temporal augment.

Second Aorist Middle Indicative and Infinitive

The stem of the aorist middle is the same as that of the aorist active (the third principal part of the verb minus the -ον ending). To this stem, the secondary middle-passive endings are added with the intervention of a thematic vowel as follows:

singular	person	plural
ἐ-λιπ-ό-μην	1	ἐ-λιπ-ό-μεθα
I left (for) myself		*We left (for) ourselves*
ἐ-λίπ-ου	2	ἐ-λίπ-ε-σθε
You left (for) yourself		*You left (for) yourselves*
ἐ-λίπ-ε-το	3	ἐ-λίπ-ο-ντο
He/She/It left (for)		*They left (for) themselves*
him-/her-/itself		

Infinitive   λιπ-έ-σθαι
To leave (for) oneself

Notes: Here again, in the second person singular, intervocalic sigma has dropped out, causing the form to contract as follows:

ἐλίπε[σ]ο → ἐλίπεο → ἐλίπου

The second aorist middle infinitive is accented on the penult in spite of its short ultima.

Vocabulary

δέχομαι, δέξομαι, ἐδεξάμην, ____, δέδεγμαι, ἐδέχθην *receive, accept*

ἕπομαι, ἕψομαι, ἑσπόμην (aor. inf. σπέσθαι), ____, ____, ____ (+ dative) *follow*

τρέπω, τρέψω, ἔτρεψα, τέτροφα, τέτραμμαι, ἐτράπην (intransitive in the middle voice) *turn* (apotropaic)

ἐπεί *when, since*

ἐπειδή *when, since*

ἕως *as long as, until*

ἐκεῖνος, ἐκείνη, ἐκεῖνο *that*

ὅδε, ἥδε, τόδε (often refers to what follows) *this*

οὗτος, αὕτη, τοῦτο (often refers to what precedes) *this*

Drill A

Give the following forms and translate:

1. οὗτος ὁ to agree with:
   ὁδός, ἥλιος, οἰκίαι, δῶρα, γνωμῶν

2. ἐκεῖνος ὁ to agree with:
   παιδίον, χρόνον, νήσῳ, διαβολάς, λίθου

3. ὅδε ὁ to agree with:
   ποταμῶν, χρυσίον, χῶραι, στρατιαῖς, βιβλία

Drill B

Conjugate:

1. aorist middle of ἕπομαι, τρέπω
2. future middle of δέχομαι, φεύγω
3. aorist active of λαμβάνω, σώζω

Drill C

Supply the form of the pronoun to translate the English word(s) in parentheses and, if possible, make the pronoun agree with the noun provided; translate the completed phrase:

1. (those) τοῖς πολέμοις

2. τῆς εἰρήνης (this, use οὗτος)

3. (that) τῷ οἴνῳ

4. (those things, acc.) ἔπαθον.

5. τὰ (their) δῶρα λήψει.

6. (these, use ὅδε) τὰ παιδία

7. αἱ ὁδοί (these, use οὗτος)

8. (this, use ὅδε) τὸ χρυσίον

9. (them, use οὗτος) ἑψόμεθα.

10. (this, use οὗτος) τὸν νέον ἐφύγομεν.

Drill D

Translate:

1. They received
2. He began
3. I deliberated
4. I will listen
5. She will provide
6. I turn (i.e. myself)
7. You (sg.) follow
8. We fled
9. You stop yourselves
10. They saved themselves

Exercise A

Translate:

1. ἐθέλετε τούτῳ τῷ στρατηγῷ σπέσθαι εἰς ἐκείνην τὴν χώραν;
2. οἱ ἀθάνατοι θεοὶ οὐ δέξονται τὰ τῶν ἀδίκων δῶρα.
3. ἐπεὶ οἱ πρῶτοι ἄνθρωποι εἰς οἶνον ἐτρέψαντο, δεινὰ ἔπαθον.
4. οἱ μὲν μέλλουσι τοῖς δικαίοις ἕψεσθαι καὶ τὴν τιμὴν δέξεσθαι· οἱ δὲ μέλλουσι τοῖς ἀδίκοις πείσεσθαι, ἐπειδὴ πλούτῳ καὶ οἴνῳ ἄρχονται.
5. ἐκεῖνος ὁ στρατηγὸς τὴν στρατιὰν ἔπεισε δέξασθαι τὸ χρυσίον καὶ σῶσαι τὸν υἱὸν εἰς τὴν τῶν φίλων χώραν.

Exercise B

Translate:

1. Until we seized the gold, we were willing to suffer those terrible dangers.
2. Since these men wished to educate their sons, they turned their thoughts to the books of the wise.
3. Those children did not wish to obey their brothers.
4. When the general came into the market-place, he stopped and said these things.
5. That large house on the island is being guarded by many.

Lesson 13

Imperfect Active and Middle-Passive Indicative
Contrary-to-Fact Conditions

Imperfect Active and Middle-Passive Indicative

The imperfect tense expresses a continuous action (Example: "I was educating") or repeated action (Example: "I used to educate" or "I kept on educating") in past time. When the imperfect expresses a single act, as it often does (Example: "I educated"), it represents that act in progress. Thus, the imperfect has a progressive aspect (i.e. like a video), unlike the aorist which has a simple aspect (i.e. like a digital snapshot) (see Lesson 8).

The imperfect stem is found by dropping the -ω from the end of the first principal part of the verb and then augmenting that stem in the same manner as in the aorist tense (see Lesson 8). The endings added to this stem are the same as those of the <u>second</u> aorist, in both the active and middle-passive voices (see Lesson 8).

Active:

singular	person	plural
ἐ-παίδευ-ο-ν *I was educating*	1	ἐ-παιδεύ-ο-μεν *We were educating*
ἐ-παίδευ-ε-ς *You (sing.) were educating*	2	ἐ-παιδεύ-ε-τε *You (pl.) were educating*
ἐ-παίδευ-ε *He/She/It was educating*	3	ἐ-παίδευ-ο-ν *They were educating*

Middle-Passive:

singular	person	plural
ἐ-παιδευ-ό-μην *I was educating (for) myself* (mid.) *I was being educated* (pass.)	1	ἐ-παιδευ-ό-μεθα *We were educating (for) ourselves* (mid.) *We were being educated* (pass.)
ἐ-παιδεύ-ου *You were educating (for)* *yourself* (mid.) *You were being educated* (pass.)	2	ἐ-παιδεύ-ε-σθε *You were educating (for)* *yourselves* (mid.) *You were being educated* (pass.)
ἐ-παιδεύ-ε-το *He/She/It was educating* *(for) him-/her-/itself* (mid.) *He/She/It was being educated* (pass.)	3	ἐ-παιδεύ-ο-ντο *They were educating (for)* *themselves* (mid.) *They were being educated* (pass.)

Note: The imperfect of ἔχω is εἶχον, εἶχες, εἶχε, etc. The imperfect of ἕπομαι is εἱπόμην, εἵπου, εἵπετο, etc.

Contrary-to-Fact Conditions

Conditions are made up of a subordinate "if" clause, known as the protasis, and a main clause, known as the apodosis. Example:

If it is raining (protasis), I will carry my umbrella (apodosis).

There are many types of conditions, depending on the time to which the conditions refer and the likelihood that they may be realized. Conditions which contain a supposition impossible to fulfill are called contrary-to-fact conditions. They are divided into two categories according to the time to which they refer. Present contrary-to-fact conditions contain suppositions contrary to the facts of the moment. Past contrary-to-fact conditions contain suppositions contrary to the facts of the past. These conditions are formed and translated as follows:

	Protasis (negated by μή)	Apodosis (negated by οὐ)
Contrary-to-fact Present:	εἰ + imperfect indicative	imperfect indicative + ἄν
	If … were	would
Example:	εἰ τῆς χώρας ἦρχον, ἔπαυον ἂν τὸν πόλεμον.	
	If I were ruling the country, I would stop the war.	
Contrary-to-fact Past:	εἰ + aorist indicative	aorist indicative + ἄν
	If … had	would have
Example:	εἰ τῆς χώρας ἦρξα, οὐκ ἂν ἔπαυσα τὸν πόλεμον.	
	If I had ruled the country, I would not have stopped the war.	

Notes: In contrary-to-fact conditions, the imperfect and aorist indicative are not translated as they are in other types of sentences. Therefore, it is important both to recognize the presence of a conditional sentence and identify the type of condition before translating.

The adverb ἄν, used in the apodoses of contrary-to-fact conditions, is postpositive, meaning that it cannot stand as the first word in its clause. There is no standard translation for ἄν; however, its presence in a Greek sentence typically indicates – as in a contrary-to-fact condition – that something contra factual or less than real is occurring.

When the protasis of a contrary-to-fact condition refers to one time and the apodosis to another, a "mixed" condition occurs. Example:

εἰ μὴ ὁ στρατηγὸς ἔλυσε τὴν ὁδὸν ἐκείνην, τὸν κίνδυνον ἂν ἔφευγε.
If the general had __not__ destroyed that road, he would (now) be fleeing the danger.

Vocabulary

θάπτω, θάψω, ἔθαψα, ____, τέθαμμαι, ἐτάφην *bury* (epitaph)

φείδομαι, φείσομαι, ἐφεισάμην, ____, ____, ____ (+ genitive) *spare*

Ἀθηναῖος, -ου, ὁ *Athenian*

ἰατρός, -οῦ, ὁ *doctor*
 (pediatrician)

νίκη, -ης, ἡ *victory* (epinician)

νόμος, -ου, ὁ *law, custom*
 (astronomy)

ξένος, -ου, ὁ *guest-friend,*
 stranger (xenophobia)

σύμμαχος, -ου, ὁ *ally*

ἐκ (ἐξ before vowels) (+
 genitive) *out of, from*

εἰ *if*

μή *not*

ἄν (postpositive adverb –
 untranslatable)

Drill A   P#T V M : Trans

Parse and translate:

1. ἐλείπετε *y'all were leaving*
2. ἐλίπετε *y'all left*
3. ἐθάψαμεν *We buried*
4. ἐθάπτομεν *We were burying*
5. μέλλει φείσεσθαι
6. εἵποντο *they*
7. φείδει
8. ἐφείδου
9. ἔφευγε
10. ἔφυγε

Drill B

Change the voice of the verbs as indicated in parentheses; translate the result:

1. ἐπείθομεν (middle)
2. πάσχονται (active)
3. ἦρχες (passive)
4. τρέπουσι (middle)
5. ἐπιστευσάμην (active)
6. ἔθαπτον, singular (passive)

Drill C

Change the following verbs to the imperfect tense; translate the result:

1. φείδομαι
2. ἕσπετο
3. λήψεσθε
4. δέξει
5. ἐφύγου
6. διαφθείρονται

Drill D

Determine whether the following English sentences are examples of contrary-to-fact conditions. For those which are contrary-to-fact conditions, write the formula (i.e. tense and mood of the verbs, etc.) that would be used to translate the sentences into Greek:

1. I would take the challenge, if you were offering it.
2. If I am going to be last in line, I don't want to wait at all.
3. If we had noticed earlier, it would not have been so much trouble.
4. I always do my best, if ever I am needed.
5. If I were in your shoes, I'd do something very different.
6. If you had come for help, you would have been better off.

Exercise A

Translate:

1. εἰ μὴ τοῦ σοφοῦ ἠκούετε, εἵπεσθε ἂν τούτῳ τῷ ξένῳ.
2. διὰ τὴν δεινὴν νόσον οἱ ἰατροὶ ἠθέλησαν πέμψαι τὰ παιδία ἐκ τῆς χώρας.
3. εἰ ἐμέλλησας φείσεσθαι ἐκείνου τοῦ σοφοῦ, οὐκ ἂν ἤκουσας τῶν ἀδίκων συμμάχων.
4. τῷ γὰρ νόμῳ ἄρχονται οἱ ἄνθρωποι καὶ ὑπὸ τῶν θεῶν.
5. οἱ Ἀθηναῖοι ἔπαθον ἂν πολλὰ κακὰ καὶ δεινά, εἰ μὴ ἐβουλεύσαντο καὶ τὸν πόλεμον ἔπαυσαν.

Exercise B

Translate:

1. If that woman were obeying the law, she would not be burying her brother.
2. As long as the allies trusted that general, he avoided danger.
3. If we had obeyed the Athenians, we would have spared the children.
4. By means of this victory the general was persuading many Athenians to leave their friends and follow the expedition.
5. If he had received the stranger into his house, he would not have suffered an evil death at the hands of the god.

Lesson 14

εἰμί (Indicative and Infinitive Forms). Enclitics.
Predicate Nouns and Adjectives

εἰμί

The irregular verb εἰμί, "I am," is conjugated as follows:

Present Indicative

singular	person	plural
εἰμί	1	ἐσμέν
I am		*We are*
εἶ	2	ἐστέ
You are		*You are*
ἐστί(ν)	3	εἰσί(ν)
He/She/It is		*They are*

Infinitive εἶναι *to be*

Future Indicative

singular	person	plural
ἔσομαι	1	ἐσόμεθα
I shall be		*We shall be*
ἔσει (-η)	2	ἔσεσθε
You will be		*You will be*
ἔσται	3	ἔσονται
He/She/It will be		*They will be*

Infinitive ἔσεσθαι *to be about to be*
Note: the third person singular form, ἔσται, lacks a thematic vowel.

Imperfect Indicative

singular	person	plural
ἦ or ἦν	1	ἦμεν
I was		*We were*
ἦσθα	2	ἦτε
You were		*You were*
ἦν	3	ἦσαν
He/She/It was		*They were*

Enclitics

An enclitic is a word closely associated with the word which <u>precedes</u> it; such a word, as suggested by its etymology, "leans" (κλίν-) "on" (ἐν) the word behind it. It may lose or retain its accent in accordance with the rules listed below. All forms of the <u>present</u> indicative of εἰμί <u>except</u> the second person singular (εἶ) are enclitics. The enclitics in the examples below will be underlined.

a (1).   An enclitic <u>loses</u> its accent when it follows a word accented on the <u>ultima</u>. In this situation, the acute or circumflex accent of the preceding word remains unchanged:

δεινοί <u>τε</u> καὶ κακοί <u>ἐστε</u>.
You are both clever and wicked.

Here the enclitics τέ and ἐστέ lose their accents because the words they follow, δεινοί and κακοί respectively, both have an accented ultima. Furthermore, the acute accents of δεινοί and κακοί, which stand on the ultima, remain unchanged; were they not followed by the enclitics τέ and ἐστέ, the acute accents of δεινοί and κακοί would have changed to grave accents.

<u>Note</u>: τέ is an enclitic often used in conjunction with καί to mean "<u>both</u> ... <u>and</u>." It always appears immediately <u>after</u> the first element of a correlated pair of words, as in the example above.

(2).   An enclitic "<u>donates</u>" its acute accent to the ultima of the word which it follows when that word is a proclitic, another enclitic, or a word with an acute accent on the <u>antepenult</u> or a circumflex on the <u>penult</u>. Examples:

οἵ <u>τε</u> δίκαιοι καὶ οἱ ἄδικοι κακὰ ἔπαθον.
Both the just and the unjust suffered evil.

Here the enclitic τέ "donates" its acute accent to the ultima of the normally unaccented proclitic οἱ.

σύμμαχός <u>ἐστί</u> <u>τε</u> καὶ ἦν.
He both is and was an ally.

Here the enclitic τέ "donates" its acute accent to the ultima of the enclitic ἐστί, which in turn donates its acute to σύμμαχος, a word with an acute accent on the antepenult.

τὸ δῶρόν <u>ἐστι</u> καλόν.
The gift is beautiful.

Here the enclitic ἐστί "donates" its acute accent to the ultima of δῶρον, a word with a circumflex accent on the ultima.

b.   An enclitic with two syllables <u>retains</u> its accent (always on the
ultima) when it follows a word with an acute accent on the
penult. A monosyllabic enclitic, however, <u>loses</u> its accent in this
situation. Examples:

φίλοι ἐσμέν.
We are friends.

Here the <u>two-syllable</u> enclitic ἐσμέν retains its accent since it
follows φίλοι, a word with an acute accent on the penult.

φίλος τε καὶ σύμμαχος εἶ
You are both a friend and an ally.

Here the <u>one-syllable</u> enclitic τέ loses its accent since it follows
φίλοι, a word with an acute accent on the penult.

<u>Note</u>: Enclitics are always used postpositively.

<u>Predicate Nouns and Adjectives</u>

All nouns and adjectives that stand in the predicate of a sentence and
explain or describe the subject of the verb must be placed in the same case as the
subject. In the examples that follow, the predicate adjectives are underlined.

Both εἰμί and γίγνομαι tend to take predicate nominatives, since they
define or describe the subject rather than indicate that the subject is acting on
someone or something else:

οἱ θεοί εἰσιν <u>ἀθάνατοι</u>   τὰ παιδία γίγνεται <u>καλά</u>.
The gods are <u>immortal</u>.   *The children are becoming <u>beautiful</u>.*

<u>Note</u>: As was noted in a similar example from Lesson 9, it is not unusual for Greek
to eliminate the verb "to be" altogether. Thus, οἱ θεοί ἀθάνατοι would also be
translated "the gods are immortal." Greek typically differentiates the subject from
the predicate by applying an article to the subject, as <u>οἱ</u> θεοί above.

<u>Vocabulary</u>

γίγνομαι, γενήσομαι, ἐγενόμην, γέγονα, γεγένημαι, _____ *become; be;
happen; prove to be; be born* (genesis)

διδάσκω, διδάξω, ἐδίδαξα, δεδίδαχα, δεδίδαγμαι, ἐδιδάχθην (+ two
accusatives) *teach* (didactic)

εἰμί, ἔσομαι, ____, ____, ____, ____ *be*

πορεύομαι, πορεύσομαι, ἐπορευσάμην, _____, πεπόρευμαι,
ἐπορεύθην *go, march, proceed, advance*

πράττω, πράξω, ἔπραξα, πέπραχα, πέπραγμαι, ἐπράχθην *do; make; achieve* (practical)

σφάττω, σφάξω, ἔσφαξα, _____, ἔσφαγμαι, ἐσφάγην *slay, kill*

τε ... καί *both ... and*

περί (+ genitive) *about, concerning*
   (+ accusative) *about, around* (periscope)

παρά (+ genitive) *from (the side of)* (parallel)
   (+ dative) *at (the side of)*
   (+ accusative) *to (the side of); along (the side of); contrary to*

εὖ (adverb) *well* (euphemism, euphony)

κακῶς (adverb) *badly*

εὖ πράττειν *(to) fare well*

κακῶς πράττειν *(to) fare badly*

Ἀθῆναι, -ῶν, αἱ *Athens*

Note: διδάσκω governs <u>two</u> direct objects in the accusative case. Example:

ὁ σοφὸς τοὺς νέους τὴν ἀρετὴν ἐδίδαξεν.
The wise man taught the young men excellence.

Drill A

Copy, accent correctly, and translate:

1. ἄνθρωπος εἰμι.
2. ὁ οἶνος ἐστι κακος.
3. ἀθανατοι τε και σοφοι ἐσμεν.
4. ἀδικοι εἰσιν.
5. ξενοι ἐστε.

Drill B

Parse and translate:

1. ἐγιγνόμην
2. ἐγενόμην
3. πορεύσει
4. εἶ
5. γενέσθαι

6. ἔσφαττεν
7. ἔσφαξεν
8. ἦ
9. διδάξαι
10. ἔσται

Drill C

Change the verb form as indicated in parentheses; translate the result:

1. λείψονται (aorist)
2. ἐστέ (future)
3. ἤκουες (plural)
4. ἐλύσω (active)
5. εσπεύσαντο (active)

6. ἦσαν (singular)
7. εὖ πράττομεν (middle)
8. ἔσομαι (plural)
9. διδάξειν (present)
10. γενήσομαι (aorist)

Drill D

Translate:

1. I was *η*
2. They became *εγενοντον*
3. He will be *εσται*

4. To be *ειναι*
5. I was making *επραττον*
6. I fared badly *κακως εποαξα*

Exercise A

Translate:

1. ἡ μεγάλη στρατιὰ ἐπορεύετο παρὰ τὸν ποταμὸν καὶ εἰς τὴν ὁδὸν ἔσπευδεν.

2. εἰ περὶ τοῦ ἐκείνου τοῦ φίλου θανάτου ἤκουσα, εἰς τὴν ἀγορὰν ἄν ἔσπευσα καὶ ἐκεῖνον ἄν ἔθαψα.

3. οὗτος ὁ στρατηγὸς ἐκέλευσε τὴν στρατιὰν παρὰ τῇ ὁδῷ παύσασθαι.

4. τάδε τὰ δῶρά ἐστι πολλά τε καὶ καλά.

5. εἰ μὴ ἐγενόμην, οὐκ ἂν ἔπραττον κακῶς.

Exercise B

Translate:

1. When they stopped the doctor at the side of the road, they seized his gold and slew his friends.

2. We are both just and worthy of honor.

3. When terrible things were happening around Athens, we brought our children safely out of danger.

4. If the Athenians had not slain their generals, they would have fared well; for the gods would have made peace and stopped the terrible war.

5. In time a child will be born and he will save the souls of both the just and the unjust.

Lesson 15

Review

Drill A

Give the following forms; translate:

1. nominative plural of:
   αὕτη ἡ νῆσος, τὸ βιβλίον τοῦτο, ὅδε ὁ πλοῦτος
2. dative singular of:
   ἐκείνη ἡ ὁδός, ὁ ἄδικος φίλος οὗτος,
   τόδε τὸ δῶρον
3. accusative plural of:
   αἱ καλαὶ Ἀθῆναι, οὗτος ὁ ἰατρός,
   ἐκεῖνο τὸ παιδίον

Drill B

Parse and translate the following forms:

1. ἐπράξω		6. εἵπετο	
2. πράξω		7. ἕσπετο	
3. ἦγες		8. ἔσει	
4. εἶναι		9. εἴχομεν	
5. ἤγαγες		10. ἐδίδαξαν	

Drill C

Synopsis Drill. A synopsis of a verb groups together all tenses of that verb in a given mood or moods in the same person and number. For example, a synopsis of παιδεύω in the first person singular, in the indicative mood would appear as follows:

	Active	Middle/Passive	Middle
Present	παιδεύω	παιδεύομαι	
Imperfect	ἐπαίδευον	ἐπαιδευόμην	
Future	παιδεύσω		παιδεύσομαι
Aorist	ἐπαίδευσα		ἐπαιδευσάμην

Give synopses of the following verbs in the active and middle voices, wherever possible:

1. ἔχω in the first person plural
2. εἰμί in the third person plural
3. ἀκούω in the third person singular
4. γίγνομαι in the second person singular

Drill D

For each of the following verbs, give all infinitives studied:

1. βουλεύω   2. λείπω

Exercise A

Translate:

1. ἐπειδὴ οἱ Ἀθηναῖοι τοὺς νέους τὴν ἀρετὴν ἐδίδασκον ἤκουον καὶ πολλοὶ ξένοι.
2. εἰ θεὸς ἦν, τοὺς ἀδίκους εἶναι δικαίους ἐδίδασκον ἄν.
3. εἰ κακὰ ἔπραττον οἱ Ἀθηναῖοι, οὐκ ἂν ἦσαν ἄξιοι τιμῆς.
4. μετὰ τοῦ θεοῦ εὖ πράξομεν καὶ τρέψομεν τὸν πόλεμον εἰς τὴν εἰρήνην.
5. εἰ μὲν οἱ υἱοὶ οἱ ἐκείνου τοῦ ξένου ἐγένοντο ἵπποι, τούτους ἂν ἐδίδαξε τὴν τῶν ἵππων ἀρετήν· ἐπεὶ δὲ ἄνθρωποί εἰσιν, τούτους ἐδίδαξε τὴν τῶν ἀνθρώπων ἀρετήν.

Exercise B

Translate:

1. The sun is an immortal god in the sky.
2. Because of their excellence those Athenians will become worthy of honor.
3. Great books about justice and honor are written by great men.
4. Even if the Athenians had followed their generals into danger, they would have suffered at the hands of their allies.
5. The generals of the Athenians will order their friends to guard the gold of their allies.

Lesson 16

Personal Pronouns. αὐτός. Elision and Crasis. Expressions of Possibility

Personal Pronouns (First and Second Persons)

The personal pronouns of the first and second persons are declined as follows:

First Person:		Second Person:	
singular	plural	singular	plural
ἐγώ	ἡμεῖς	σύ	ὑμεῖς
I	*we*	*you*	*you*
ἐμοῦ (μου)	ἡμῶν	σοῦ (σου)	ὑμῶν
of me	*of us*	*of you*	*of you*
ἐμοί (μοι)	ἡμῖν	σοί (σοι)	ὑμῖν
to/for me	*to/for us*	*to/for you*	*to/for you*
ἐμέ (με)	ἡμᾶς	σέ (σε)	ὑμᾶς
me	*us*	*you*	*you*

Note: The <u>unaccented</u> forms of the first and second persons are <u>enclitics</u> (see Lesson 14) and are more commonly used than the <u>accented</u> forms, which are <u>emphatic</u>. <u>Emphatic</u> forms, however, are used with prepositions.

The nominative of a personal pronoun is employed only for emphasis or contrast. Usually, the ending of a verb is sufficient to indicate the person. Example:

<u>ἐγώ</u> μὲν δίκαιός εἰμι, <u>σὺ</u> δὲ κακὸς εἶ.
I am just, but <u>you</u> are evil.

Declension of αὐτός

singular

	masculine	feminine	neuter
Nom.	αὐτός	αὐτή	αὐτό
Gen.	αὐτοῦ	αὐτῆς	αὐτοῦ
Dat.	αὐτῷ	αὐτῇ	αὐτῷ
Acc.	αὐτόν	αὐτήν	αὐτό

	plural		
Nom.	αὐτοί	αὐταί	αὐτά
Gen.	αὐτῶν	αὐτῶν	αὐτῶν
Dat.	αὐτοῖς	αὐταῖς	αὐτοῖς
Acc.	αὐτούς	αὐτάς	αὐτά

Uses of αὐτός

a. Personal Pronoun

As a personal pronoun of the third person, αὐτός is used <u>only</u> in the oblique cases (i.e., genitive, dative and accusative). It is the most common form of the third person pronoun, appearing in this sense more frequently than οὗτος, ὅδε, or ἐκεῖνος. Example:

<u>αὐτοὺς</u> ἔπεισά μοι ἕπεσθαι.
I persuaded <u>them</u> to follow me.

<u>Note</u>: Used as a possessive ("his," "her," "its"; "their"), αὐτός stands in <u>predicate</u> position, unlike the demonstratives (see Lesson 12). Example:

οἱ σύμμαχοι <u>αὐτῶν</u> ἐβουλεύοντο περὶ τῆς νίκης ὑμῶν.
<u>Their</u> allies were deliberating about your victory.

b. Intensive Pronoun

As an intensive pronoun meaning "-self," αὐτός appears in the <u>predicate</u> position. It is used in all grammatical cases to intensify any word or emphasize any person or number. Examples:

ἔσωσα <u>αὐτὸς</u> τὸν στρατηγόν.
I <u>myself</u> saved the general.

ἔσωσα τὸν στρατηγὸν <u>αὐτόν</u>.
I saved the general <u>himself</u>.

ἠκούσατέ μου καὶ <u>αὐτοί</u>.
Even you <u>yourselves</u> heard me.

c. Identifying Adjective

As an adjective meaning "same," αὐτός appears in the <u>attributive</u> position. Example:

τοῖς <u>αὐτοῖς</u> νόμοις ἀρχόμεθα.
We are ruled by the <u>same</u> laws.

Elision and Crasis

a. <u>Elision</u>: To avoid hiatus (i.e. a succession of vowels), Greek uses <u>elision</u>, i.e., the removal of a short, unaccented vowel at the end of a word before a word beginning with a vowel. Example:

ἐλθεῖν οἷοί τ᾽ ἦσαν (= τε ἦσαν).

They were able to come.

b. <u>Crasis:</u> Often a vowel or diphthong at the end of a word is fused with one at the beginning of the following word. This fusion of two words, called <u>crasis,</u> is identified by the breathing which remains on the second word after the fusion has occurred. Example:

κἀγὼ (= καὶ ἐγώ) ταῦτα ταὐτὰ (= τὰ αὐτὰ) ἔπαθον.

I, too, suffered these same things.

Expressions of Possibility

Like English, which can express possibility in a variety of ways, such as "I am able to run," "I can run," "It is possible for me to run," Greek also has many ways of expressing possibility.

a. Personal constructions:

(1). subject + οἷός τε, οἵα τε, οἷόν τε + form of εἶναι + infinitive

Examples: ὁ ἄνθρωπος οἷός τέ ἐστι λέγειν
              The man is able to speak
              <u>Note</u>: οἷός τε is equivalent to the English word "able." Like
              any other adjective in Greek, οἷός must agree with the subject of
              the sentence in gender, number, and case. οἷός is declined like
              an adjective of the first and second declensions. The enclitic τε
              does not decline.

(2). subject + form of ἔχω + infinitive

Example: ὁ ἄνθρωπος ἔχει λέγειν
         The man is able to speak
         literally: *The man has (the ability) to speak*

b. Impersonal constructions:

(1). (ἔξ)εστι(ν) + dative (of person) + infinitive

Example: ἔστι τῷ ἀνθρώπῳ λέγειν
It is possible for the man to speak
literally: *It (i.e. the possibility) exists for the man to speak*

(2). οἷόν τέ + ἐστι + dative (of person) + infinitive
Example: οἷόν τέ ἐστι τῷ ἀνθρώπῳ λέγειν
It is possible for the man to speak
Note: As the subject in this construction is always the
impersonal "it," the neuter singular form οἷόν τε is always used.

Vocabulary

διώκω, διώξω, ἐδίωξα, δεδίωκα, _____, ἐδιώχθην *pursue; prosecute*

ἔξεστι(ν) (+ dative) *it is possible*

ἔστι(ν) (an emphatic form, with accented penult, knows as "existential" ἔστι;
+ dative) *it is possible*

ἔχω (+ infinitive) *be able, can*

οἷός τε, οἷα τε, οἷόν τε εἶναι (+ infinitive) *be able, can*

κωλύω, κωλύσω, ἐκώλυσα, κεκώλυκα, κεκώλυμαι, ἐκωλύθην *hinder,
prevent*

μέμφομαι, μέμψομαι, ἐμεμψάμην, _____, _____, ἐμέμφθην *blame, find
fault with*

ψεύδω, ψεύσω, ἔψευσα, _____, ἔψευσμαι, ἐψεύσθην *deceive;* (in the
middle voice) *lie* (pseudonym)

μή (negative adverb used with   ἐγώ *I;* ἡμεῖς *we* (egoist)
infinitives) *not*
                                       σύ *you* (sing.); ὑμεῖς *you* (pl.)

αὐτός, -ή, -ό (third person pronoun in oblique cases) *his, (to/for/of)* him,
(to/for/of) her, its, *(to/for/of)* it, etc. (sing.); *their, (to/for/of)* them, etc. (pl.);
(intensive pronoun in all cases in predicate position)-*self;*
(in attributive position) *same* (autodidact, autograph, automobile)

Note: κωλύω often takes an objective infinitive <u>with or without</u> μή Here μή is
not a negative; it is best translated as "from." Examples:

ἐκωλύσαμεν αὐτοὺς μὴ κακῶς πρᾶξαι.
We prevented them from faring badly.

ἐκωλύσαμεν αὐτοὺς κακῶς πρᾶξαι.
We prevented them from faring badly.

Drill A

Identify the form of αὐτός as a personal pronoun, an intensive pronoun, or an identifying adjective; translate:

1. οἱ αὐτοὶ ἄνθρωποι μέμφονται ὑμᾶς.
2. ὁ ἰατρὸς αὐτὸς εὖ πραττει.
3. ὁ στρατηγὸς αὐτοὺς ἔσφαξεν.
4. αὐταὶ εἰς Ἀθῆνας ἐλεύσονται.
5. ἐγὼ μετὰ αὐτοῦ παρὰ τὸν πόταμον ἐπορευόμην.
6. τὰ καλὰ αὐτὰ ὑπὸ τῶν θεῶν αὐτῶν διδάσκεται.
7. σὺ ἐν τῇ αὐτῇ χώρᾳ εἶ;
8. οἱ σοφοὶ ἐκεῖνοι αὐτῆς ἐφείσαντο.

Drill B

Translate, then rewrite each sentence using the other three methods of expressing possibility in Greek:

1. ἔστι ὑμῖν τὸν καλὸν μέμφεσθαι;
2. οἱ θέοι αὐτοὶ οἷοί τε οὔκ εἰσι τὸν ἥλιον λύειν.
3. ἡμεῖς ἔχομεν εἰς τὸν πόταμον σπεύδειν.

Exercise A

Translate:

1. οὔκ ἔστιν ἡμῖν ὑπ᾽ αὐτῶν βλάπτεσθαι, καὶ εἰ ψεύδονται περὶ ἡμῶν.
2. οἵδε οἱ νέοι δίκαιοί εἰσιν· ἡμᾶς μὲν οὐ μέμψονται, ὑμῖν δ᾽ ἔψονταί τε καὶ πείσονται.
3. καὶ αὐτὸς οὐκ ἔσχε πεῖσαι τοὺς Ἀθηναίους σχεῖν τὴν αὐτὴν γνώμην περὶ ἐκείνου τοῦ νόμου.
4. εἴ σου τὰ παιδία ἡμῖν ἐπείσατο, αὐτοὶ παρέσχομεν ἂν δῶρα ἐκείνοις.
5. οἱ Ἀθηναῖοι αὐτοὶ οὐχ οἷοί τ᾽ ἦσαν κωλύειν τοὺς στρατηγοὺς μὴ πορεύεσθαι εἰς τοὺς τοῦ πολέμου κινδύνους.

Exercise B

Translate:

    1. Did they fare well at the hands of the gods when they buried the strangers?

    2. As long as the Athenians received gold from the same allies, they guarded their lands.

    3. If he himself were blaming me on account of these same things, he would be lying.

    4. Even I cannot persuade them not to prosecute our doctor.

    5. It is not possible for you (pl.) to save the unjust men from death contrary to the laws.

11. ὁ Σόλων τοὺς νόμους τοῖς Ἀθηναιοῖς παρεῖχε.

Lesson 17

ε-contract Verbs. Liquid Verbs

ε-contract Verbs

In verbs that have a <u>present stem</u> ending in a vowel (e.g. ποιέω *make, do*), the final vowel of that stem often contracts in the <u>present</u> and <u>imperfect</u> tenses when it encounters the vowel(s) of the verb ending. ε-contract verbs, which have a present stem ending in ε, contract according to the following rules:

1. ε + long vowel or diphthong = ε drops
2. ε + ε = ει
3. ε + ο = ου

<u>Note</u>: If the stem vowel (ε) is accented, then the vowel(s) which result(s) from the contraction receive(s) a circumflex. Example:

ποιέω = ποιῶ
<u>but</u> ἐποίεον = ἐποίουν

Present Active Indicative and Infinitive

In the charts to follow, the <u>actual</u> form of the verb is written first; the uncontracted form of the verb is written in parentheses:

<u>singular</u>	<u>person</u>	<u>plural</u>
ποιῶ (ποιέω)	1	ποιοῦμεν (ποιέομεν)
ποιεῖς (ποιέεις)	2	ποιεῖτε (ποιέετε)
ποιεῖ (ποιέει)	3	ποιοῦσι(ν) (ποιέουσι)

Infinitive ποιεῖν (ποιέειν)

Present Middle-Passive Indicative and Infinitive

<u>singular</u>	<u>person</u>	<u>plural</u>
ποιοῦμαι (ποιέουμαι)	1	ποιούμεθα (ποιεόμεθα)
ποιεῖ (ποιέει, ποιέῃ)	2	ποιεῖσθε (ποιέεσθε)
ποιεῖται (ποιέεται)	3	ποιοῦνται (ποιέονται)

Infinitive ποιεῖσθαι (ποιέεσθαι)

Note: The second person singular middle-passive forms shown in parentheses (ποιέει, ποιέῃ) are already the result of a contraction – the loss of intervocalic sigma (ποιέε[σ]αι). The final form ποιεῖ looks identical to the third person singular form of the present active indicative.

Imperfect Active Indicative

singular	person	plural
ἐποίουν (ἐποίεον)	1	ἐποιοῦμεν (ἐποιέομεν)
ἐποίεις (ἐποίεες)	2	ἐποιεῖτε (ἐποιέετε)
ἐποίει (ἐποίεε)	3	ἐποίουν (ἐποίεον)

Imperfect Middle-Passive Indicative

singular	person	plural
ἐποιούμην (ἐποιεόμην)	1	ἐποιούμεθα (ἐποιεόμεθα)
ἐποιοῦ (ἐποιέου)	2	ἐποιεῖσθε (ἐποιέεσθε)
ἐποιεῖτο (ἐποιέετο)	3	ἐποιοῦντο (ἐποιέοντο)

Note: As in the present middle-passive, the imperfect second person singular middle-passive form shown in parentheses (ἐποιέου) is already the result of a contraction – the loss of intervocalic sigma (ἐποιέε[σ]ο).

Liquid Futures

Certain verbs with <u>future active stems</u> ending in a <u>liquid</u> consonant (λ, μ, ν, ρ) have a future tense that contracts and thus conjugates identically to the present tense of an ε-contract verb. The only way to distinguish between an ε-contract and a liquid future is to identify the verb stem. If the stem comes from the first principal part, it is the present tense; if the stem comes from the second principal part, it is the future tense. Liquid futures are particularly hard to identify in context because they lack the ordinary tense sign of the future in Greek, the letter sigma, which is lost because it is intervocalic in all forms. The principal parts of a typical liquid future appear as follows:

φαίνω, <u>φανῶ</u>, ἔφηνα, etc. *show, reveal;* (mid.) *appear*

Future Active Indicative

singular	person	plural
φανῶ (φανέ[σ]ω)	1	φανοῦμεν (φανέ[σ]ομεν)
φανεῖς (φανέ[σ]εις)	2	φανεῖτε (φανέ[σ]ετε)
φανεῖ (φανέ[σ]ει)	3	φανοῦσι(ν) (φανέ[σ]ουσι(ν))

Infinitive φανεῖν (φανέ[σ]ειν)

Future Middle Indicative

singular	person	plural
φανοῦμαι (φανέ[σ]ομαι)	1	φανούμεθα (φανε[σ]όμεθα)
φανεῖ (φανέ[σ]ει, φανέ[σ]ῃ)	2	φανεῖσθε (φανέ[σ]εσθε)
φανεῖται (φανέ[σ]εται)	3	φανοῦνται (φανέ[σ]ονται)

Infinitive φανεῖσθαι (φανέ[σ]εσθαι)

Note: As above, the second person singular form of the future middle indicative for liquid futures is the result of several different contractions:

φανέσε[σ]αι → φανέ[σ]ει/ῃ → φανεῖ

Liquid Aorists

Liquid aorists verbs are a type of **first** aorists that have a liquid consonant (λ, μ, ν, ρ) rather than a σ in their aorist active endings. Examples:

φαίνω, φανῶ, ἔφηνα
διαφθείρω, διαφθερῶ, διέφθειρα, etc. *corrupt, ruin*

Note: ε-contract verbs are not necessarily liquid aorists or vice versa.

Liquid aorists are conjugated as follows:

Aorist Active Indicative			Aorist Middle Indicative		
singular	person	plural	singular	person	plural
ἔφηνα	1	ἐφήναμεν	ἐφηνάμην	1	ἐφηνάμεθα
ἔφηνας	2	ἐφήνατε	ἐφήνω	2	ἐφήνασθε
ἔφηνε(ν)	3	ἔφηναν	ἐφήνατο	3	ἐφήναντο
Infinitive φῆναι			Infinitive φήνασθαι		

☆ – ε-contract verbs *(handwritten)*

LF – liquid future
LA – liquid aorist *(handwritten)*

Vocabulary

☆ ἀδικέω, ἀδικήσω, ἠδίκησα, ἠδίκηκα, ἠδίκημαι, ἠδικήθην *injure, wrong,*
 do wrong (to)

☆ αἱρέω, αἱρήσω, εἷλον (aorist infinitive ἑλεῖν), ᾕρηκα, ᾕρημαι, ᾑρέθην LA?? *(handwritten)*
 take, seize, capture; (in the middle voice) *choose*

LF *(handwritten)* ἀποθνῄσκω, ἀποθανοῦμαι, ἀπέθανον, τέθνηκα, ____, ____ *die, be killed* LA *(handwritten)*

LF *(handwritten)* ἀποκτείνω, ἀποκτενῶ, ἀπέκτεινα, ἀπέκτονα, ____, ____ *kill* LA *(handwritten)*

☆ κατηγορέω (imperf. κατηγόρουν), κατηγορήσω, κατηγόρησα,
 κατηγόρηκα, κατηγόρημαι, κατηγορήθην (+ genitive of person,
 + accusative of thing) *accuse*

☆ ποιέω, ποιήσω, ἐποίησα, πεποίηκα, πεποίημαι, ἐποιήθην *make, do*
 (poet)

☆ ὑπισχνέομαι, ὑποσχήσομαι, ὑπεσχόμην, ____, ὑπέσχημαι, ____
 (+ future infinitive) *promise*

LF *(handwritten)* φαίνω, φανῶ, ἔφηνα, πέφηνα, πέφασμαι, ἐφάνην *show, reveal;* (in the
 middle voice) *appear* (phenomenon)

ἀδικία, -ας, ἡ *injustice, injury,*
wrong

κατηγορία, -ας, ἡ *accusation*
(category)

κατήγορος, -ου, ὁ *accuser*

φθόνος, -ου, ὁ *jealousy, envy,*
hatred

Notes: The first principal part of an ε-contract verbs is always shown in its
uncontracted form (i. e. ἀδικέω or ὑπισχνέομαι) rather than its true, contracted
form (i. e. ἀδικῶ or ὑπισχνοῦμαι) or order to distinguish ε-contract verbs clearly
from other contract verbs, like α- and ο-contract verbs, to be learned later.
   In verbs compounded with prepositions like ἀπό, διά, εἰς, ἐκ/ἐξ, ἐν,
ἐπί, κατά, μετά, παρά, περί, πρός, σύν, or ὑπό, the verb stem is
augmented, not the preposition. Examples:

ἀποθνῄσκω, ἀποθανοῦμαι, ἀπέθανον   (aor. infin. = ἀποθανεῖν)
ἀποκτείνω, ἀποκτενῶ, ἀπέκτεινα   (aor. infin. = ἀποκτεῖναι)
παρέχω, παρέξω, παρέσχον   (aor. infin. = παρασχεῖν)
ὑπισχνέομαι, ὑποσχήσομαι, ὑπεσχόμην (aor. infin. = ὑποσχέσθαι)

Drill A

Give synopses (see Lesson 15) of the following verbs in the active and middle voices:

    1. αἱρέω in the third person plural
    2. φαίνω in the second person singular

Drill B

Parse and translate the following forms:

    1. ποιοῦσι   6. ἑλεῖν
    2. ὑπισχνεῖται   7. ἐφήνω
    3. ἀποθανούμεθα   8. φανεῖσθαι
    4. ἀποκτενοῦμεν   9. ἀποκτεῖναι
    5. ᾑρεῖτε   10. ὑπέσχου

Drill C

Change the verb form as indicated in parentheses; translate the result:

    1. ποιεῖσθαι (active)   6. ἔφαινες (aorist)
    2. ἠδίκουν, sing. (passive) 7. κατηγορεῖτε (singular)
    3. ἔφηνε (future)   8. ὑποσχήσεσθε (singular)
    4. κατηγορῆσαι (present) 9. εἵλομεν (middle)
    5. φανοῦνται (active)   10. ἀποθανεῖ (plural)

Exercise A

Translate:

    1. μέλλει εἰς ἐκείνην τὴν νῆσον σπεύσειν καὶ τοὺς δικαίους ἀποκτενεῖν.
    2. οἱ μὲν ᾑροῦντο ἀποθανεῖν· οἱ δ' ᾑροῦντο ἀδικίαν φυγεῖν καὶ τοὺς βίους σώσασθαι.
    3. οὐκ ἔστιν ἀδικεῖν καὶ εὖ πράττειν ὑπὸ τῶν θεῶν.
    4. οἵδε οἱ κατήγοροι ἐφαίνοντο εἶναι δεινοὶ λέγειν· ἐπεὶ δέ μου ἀδικίαν κατηγόρουν, ἐψεύδοντο.
    5. οὗτος ὁ Ἀθηναῖος ἀδικεῖ καὶ διαφθείρει τοὺς νέους καὶ διδάσκει αὐτοὺς μὴ πείθεσθαι τοῖς ἀθανάτοις θεοῖς.

Exercise B

Translate:

    1. As long as they obeyed me, I promised them many things.

    2. Because of (their) jealousy the gods killed that handsome stranger, for he wished to become immortal.

    3. Even a god cannot make evil men just.

    4. Reason will show the injustice of these accusations and the slander of the accusers themselves.

    5. Do you (sg.) promise to prevent the Athenian from being killed?

12. ὄστρακα. Nominated for exile are (1) Pericles, son of Xanthippus, (2) Kimon, son of Miltiades, and (3) Aristeides, son of Lysimachus.

Lesson 18

Feminine and Masculine Nouns of the First Declension (Category II and III)
Dative of Possessor

Nouns of the First Declension

First declension nouns in Greek are divided into three distinct categories, I, II, and III, based on their nominative endings. These categories can be further subdivided into "a" and "b types." The stem of "b types" end in ε, ι, or ρ, causing such nouns to feature α in their declensional endings in the singular.

Category Ia (e.g. ἀρετή) and Ib (e.g. οἰκία) first declension nouns have already been introduced in Lesson 7. These nouns are distinguished by having the long vowels -η (Ia) and -ᾱ (Ib) as endings in the nominative singular.

Category II first declension nouns, seen below, feature a <u>short</u> -ᾰ in the nominative singular. IIa nouns (e.g. θάλαττα below) retain ᾰ for the endings of the <u>nominative</u> and <u>accusative singular</u>, but shift to -η for the endings of the <u>genitive</u> and <u>dative singular</u>. Category IIb nouns (e.g. μοῖρα below) retain α throughout their singular forms, since, like all "b type" first declensions, their stems ends in ε, ι, or ρ. Ib and IIb first declension nouns do not differ at all in terms of <u>appearance</u>, but they do differ in terms of the <u>quantity</u> of their α, long for Ib and short for IIb.

Category IIIa (e.g. πολίτης below) and IIIb (e.g. νεανίας below) first declension nouns, besides ending in -ης or -ας in the nominative singular, are also distinguished by the fact that they are <u>masculine</u> in gender. All category III first declension nouns also feature -ου in the genitive singular. Like all other "b types," IIIb words like νεανίας feature α wherever possible in their singular declensional endings.

	"Type a" singular		"Type b" singular
Category I:	ἡ ἀρετή	Nom.	ἡ οἰκία
	τῆς ἀρετῆς	Gen.	τῆς οἰκίας
	τῇ ἀρετῇ	Dat.	τῇ οἰκίᾳ
	τὴν ἀρετήν	Acc.	τὴν οἰκίαν
	plural αἱ ἀρεταί	Nom.	plural αἱ οἰκίαι
	τῶν ἀρετῶν	Gen.	τῶν οἰκιῶν
	ταῖς ἀρεταῖς	Dat.	ταῖς οἰκίαις
	τὰς ἀρετάς	Acc.	τὰς οἰκίας

Category II:

	singular		singular
	ἡ θάλαττα	Nom.	ἡ μοῖρα
	τῆς θαλάττης	Gen.	τῆς μοίρας
	τῇ θαλάττῃ	Dat.	τῇ μοίρᾳ
	τὴν θάλατταν	Acc.	τὴν μοῖραν
	plural		plural
	αἱ θάλατται	Nom.	αἱ μοῖραι
	τῶν θαλαττῶν	Gen.	τῶν μοιρῶν
	ταῖς θαλάτταις	Dat.	ταῖς μοίραις
	τὰς θαλάττας	Acc.	τὰς μοίρας

Category III:

	"Type a" singular		"Type b" singular
	ὁ πολίτης	Nom.	ὁ νεανίας
	τοῦ πολίτου	Gen.	τοῦ νεανίου
	τῷ πολίτῃ	Dat.	τῷ νεανίᾳ
	τὸν πολίτην	Acc.	τὸν νεανίαν
	plural		plural
	οἱ πολῖται	Nom.	οἱ νεανίαι
	τῶν πολιτῶν	Gen.	τῶν νεανιῶν
	τοῖς πολίταις	Dat.	τοῖς νεανίαις
	τοὺς πολίτας	Acc.	τοὺς νεανίας

Notes: All first declension nouns are declined alike in the plural.

Since Category III nouns are masculine in gender, they must be modified by the masculine forms of the adjective. Examples:

τὸν δεινὸν νεανίαν ἀδικῶ.
I injure the clever young man.

ὁ καλὸς πολίτης οὐ ψεύδεται.
An honorble citizen does not lie.

Dative of Possessor

Greek frequently uses the dative case with the third person of εἰμί or γίγνομαι to indicate a possessor. In this construction, the object possessed becomes the <u>subject</u> of the Greek sentence. Examples:

αἱ ἀθάνατοι ψυχαὶ ἀνθρώποις εἰσίν.

Literally: *For men there are immortal souls;* Idiomatically: *Men have immortal souls.*

ἐμοὶ ἦν πολλὰ δῶρα.

Literally: *For me there were many gifts;* Idiomatically: *I had many gifts.*

Vocabulary

ἀλήθεια, -ας, ἡ *truth*

γέφυρα, -ας, ἡ *bridge*

δεσπότης, -ου, ὁ *master, ruler* (despot)

δικαστής, -οῦ, ὁ *judge; juror*

θάλαττα, -ης, ἡ *sea* (thalassocracy)

μοῖρα, -ας, ἡ *fate, destiny; portion*

νεανίας, -ου, ὁ *young man, youth*

πολίτης, -ου, ὁ *citizen* (politician)

στρατιώτης, -ου, ὁ *soldier*

τράπεζα, -ης, ἡ *table; bank (for money)* (trapezoid)

Drill A

Give the following forms; translate:

1. genitive singular of:
   τράπεζα, στρατιώτης, γέφυρα, νεανίας, στρατιά, ἥλιος

2. accusative singular of:
   μοῖρα, δικαστής, θάλαττα, βιβλίον, ἀλήθεια

Drill B

Give the following forms; translate:

1. οὗτος ὁ to agree with:
   δεσποτῶν, νεανίαν, στρατιώταις, τράπεζαν

Drill B (continued)

2. ἄδικος to agree with:
δεσπόται, μοίρας (gen.), στρατηγούς, δικασταῖς

3. μέγας, μεγάλη, μέγα to agree with:
διαβολῆς, ἀλήθειαν, θαλάττῃ, χωρῶν

Drill C

Put the adjective/noun pairs in the form requested; translate:

1. ἡ αὐτὴ τράπεζα (dative singular)
2. ὁ πρῶτος δικαστής (nominative plural)
3. ὁ καλὸς δεσπότης (accusative plural)
4. γέφυρα ἡ αὐτή (accusative singular)

Drill D

Translate:

1. to those jurors   3. the immortal soul (acc.)
2. a worthy fate (nom.)   4. of the evil young men

Exercise A

Translate:

1. μετὰ τὸν πόλεμον οἱ πολῖται ἀπέκτειναν ἂν
τοὺς στρατηγοὺς ἡμῶν, εἰ μὴ τοὺς σρατιώτας ἔθαψαν.
2. ἡ θάλαττά ἐστι ἡ εἰς τὸν πλοῦτον ὁδός.
3. σὺ μὲν μέλλεις ψεύσεσθαι· ἐμὲ δὲ μὴ διῶξαι τὴν
ἀλήθειαν οὐ κωλύσεις.
4. εἰ τὰς γεφύρας ἐλύσαμεν, οἱ στρατιῶται οὐκ ἂν
ἀπέθανον.
5. τῷ ἀξίῳ δικαστῇ ἦσαν τιμαί τε καὶ φίλοι.

<u>Exercise B</u>

Translate:

1. The youths took the wine from your master's table.
2. If you (pl.) were doing wrong, you would be faring badly.
3. Even the gods are ruled by fate.
4. Truth makes men immortal, but slander and envy destroy their souls.
5. A great ruler will have just laws. (Express in two ways.)

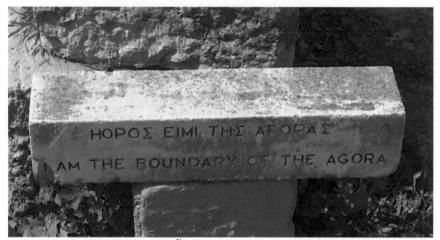

13. Boundary stone (ὅρος) of the agora, sixth century BC.

Lesson 19

α-contract Verbs. Result Clauses

α-contract Verbs

Verbs with a present stem ending in α (e.g. τιμάω *honor*), contract as follows in the present and imperfect tenses only:

1. α + ω, ου, or ο = ω
2. α + οι = ῳ
3. α + ε or η = α
4. α + ει or ῃ = ᾳ

Note: See Lesson 17 for the rules for accenting contract verbs.

Present Active Indicative and Infinitive

In the charts to follow, the actual form of the verb is written first; the uncontracted form is written in parentheses:

singular	person	plural
τιμῶ (τιμάω)	1	τιμῶμεν (τιμάομεν)
τιμᾷς (τιμάεις)	2	τιμᾶτε (τιμάετε)
τιμᾷ (τιμάει)	3	τιμῶσι(ν) (τιμάουσι)

Infinitive τιμᾶν (τιμάειν)

Present Middle-Passive Indicative and Infinitive

singular	person	plural
τιμῶμαι (τιμάομαι)	1	τιμώμεθα (τιμαόμεθα)
τιμᾷ (τιμάει, τιμάῃ)	2	τιμᾶσθε (τιμάεσθε)
τιμᾶται (τιμάεται)	3	τιμῶνται (τιμάονται)

Infinitive τιμᾶσθαι (τιμάεσθαι)

Note: Be sure to use context to differentiate the present active indicate 3rd person singular from the present middle-passive indicate 2nd person singular, the forms of which, e.g. in the case of τιμᾷ above, are identical.

Imperfect Active Indicative

singular	person	plural
ἐτίμων (ἐτίμαον)	1	ἐτιμῶμεν (ἐτιμάομεν)
ἐτίμας (ἐτίμαες)	2	ἐτιμᾶτε (ἐτιμάετε)
ἐτίμα (ἐτίμαε)	3	ἐτίμων (ἐτίμαον)

Imperfect Middle-Passive Indicative

singular	person	plural
ἐτιμώμην (ἐτιμάομην)	1	ἐτιμώμεθα (ἐτιμαόμεθα)
ἐτιμῶ (ἐτιμάου)	2	ἐτιμᾶσθε (ἐτιμάεσθε)
ἐτιμᾶτο (ἐτιμάετο)	3	ἐτιμῶντο (ἐτιμάοντο)

Result Clauses

A result clause is a subordinate clause type that indicates the outcome of the action of the main verb (e.g. I worked so hard that I did well). In Greek, ὥστε introduces result clauses. It is used with the indicative mood to denote an actual result (i.e. something that actually happens); ὥστε is used with the infinitive mood to indicate a natural or probable result (i.e. something that would or may happen). The negative with the infinitive is μή. Examples:

Actual result: οὕτω σοφός ἐστι ὥστε πολλοὶ αὐτὸν τιμῶσιν.
He is so wise that many (actually) honor him.

Natural or probable result:
οὕτω κακοί εἰσιν ὥστε ἀποκτεῖναι τοὺς ἀδελφούς.
They are so wicked that they would kill their brothers.

The infinitive in a result clause is sometimes used with a subject accusative. Example:

οὕτω λέγει ὥστε πολλοὺς αὐτῷ πιστεύειν.
He speaks in such a way that many would trust him.

Vocabulary

νικάω, νικήσω, ἐνίκησα, νενίκηκα, νενίκημαι, ἐνικήθην *conquer, win*

ὁράω (imperfect ἑώρων), ὄψομαι, εἶδον (aorist infinitive ἰδεῖν),
    ἑώρακα, ἑώραμαι, ὤφθην *see* (optics)

πειράομαι, πειράσομαι, ἐπειρασάμην, _____, πεπείραμαι, ἐπειράθην
try, attempt, endeavor

τιμάω, τιμήσω, ἐτίμησα, τετίμηκα, τετίμημαι, ἐτιμήθην *honor*

τολμάω, τολμήσω, ἐτόλμησα, τετόλμηκα, τετόλμημαι, ἐτολμήθην *dare*

χράομαι, χρήσομαι, ἐχρησάμην, _____, κέχρημαι, ἐχρήσθην (+ dative)
use; enjoy; treat; consult (an oracle) (contracts to η not α in Attic Greek)

ὥστε (+ indic.) *(so) that;*
  (+ infin.) *(so) that, (so) as (to)*

οὕτως (οὕτω before a
  consonant) *so, in such a way*

ἐπί (+ gen.) *on, upon; in the time
  of* (epithet)
  (+ dat.) *at, by; for the purpose
  of*
  (+ acc.) *to, toward; against* (in
  hostile sense)

σύν (+ dat.) *with* (synchronize)

Drill A

Give the following forms; translate:

1. imperfect active indicative, third person singular of:
    τολμάω, κατηγορέω, ὁράω, ψεύδω, αἱρέω

2. present middle indicative, third person plural of:
    χράομαι, ὑπισχνέομαι, ὁράω, ἔρχομαι, νικάω

3. imperfect middle indicative, second person singular of:
    πειράομαι, ποιέω, γίγνομαι, χράομαι, ἄγω

4. present active indicative, third person plural of:
    τιμάω, αἱρέω, φαίνω, τολμάω, ἀδικέω

5. future middle indicative, second person plural of:
    λαμβάνω, φαίνω, ὑπισχνέομαι, ἀποθνῄσκω,
    μέλλω, ἔχω

Drill B

Parse the following forms; translate:

1. ἑωρῶμεν
2. ἐχρώμην
3. ἀποκτενεῖν
4. πειρᾷ
5. ἀποθανοῦνται

6. νικᾶν
7. κατηγόρεις
8. ἐτιμᾶτε
9. διαφθερεῖ
10. ἀποκτεῖναι

Drill C

Supply the missing verb in the result clause; translate the completed
sentence:

      1. οὕτως οἱ ἄνθρωποι ἦσαν ἄδικοι, ὥστε καὶ τοῦ καλοῦ
(κατηγορέω, natural/probable result; use the aorist tense).

      2. οὕτως ἐκεῖνος ὁ ἄνθρωπος τοῖς λογοῖς χρῆται ὥστε
ὑμᾶς (πείθω, actual result; use the future tense).

      3. ὁ δεσπότης οὕτω κάκος ἐστὶ ὥστε τὸν τῶν πολίτων
πλοῦτον ἑλεῖν (τολμάω, natural/probable result; use the present tense).

Exercise A

Translate:

      1. ἐπειδὴ οἱ πρῶτοι ἄνθρωποι ἐπειρῶντο γράψασθαι,
λίθοις ἐχρῶντο· βιβλία γὰρ οὐκ ἦν αὐτοῖς.

      2. σὺν τοῖς θεοῖς οἱ τῶν Ἀθηναίων στρατηγοὶ ἐνίκησαν
τὴν παρὰ τῇ θαλάττῃ χώραν· ἀλλὰ οἱ Ἀθηναῖοι οὐκ ἐφείσαντο
αὐτῶν.

      3. ὑμεῖς οὕτω φαίνετε τὴν ἀλήθειαν ὥστε τοὺς δικαστὰς
μὴ ἐθελῆσαι ὑμᾶς βλάψαι.

      4. ἐπὶ μὲν εἰρήνης οἱ ἄνθρωποι ἀποθνῆσκουσιν ἐν ταῖς
οἰκίαις καὶ ὑπὸ τῶν φίλων θάπτονται· ἐπὶ δὲ πολέμου οὐχ οἷοι
τ᾽ εἰσι θάπτεσθαι καὶ κακὴν μοῖραν πάσχουσιν.

      5. οἱ νεανίαι οὕτως ἐχρήσαντο τῷ οἴνῳ ὥστε οὐκ εἶδον
τὸν παρὰ τῇ ὁδῷ κίνδυνον τὸν δεινόν.

Exercise B

Translate:

      1. We shall hear you (sg.), but we shall not see you (sg.).

      2. This accuser is so daring (i.e. is daring in such a way) that he
will deceive even the wise.

      3. If the ruler were honoring excellence, he would be teaching
the citizens not to do wrong.

      4. Since in my time citizens honored the gods, they fared well.

      5. When the ruler tried to advance with his allies against the
soldiers of his brother, he died by an evil fate.

Lesson 20

Review

Drill A

Translate:

1. He will have these same things. (Express in two ways.)
2. I came and buried myself.
3. He set our children free and left them on the island.
4. The same soldier was being honored.
5. The general himself is being honored because of his victory.
6. They suffered the same fate.
7. Time will reveal the truth to the judge himself.
8. I trust both you (sg.) and him.
9. He himself promises to spare us.
10. Are you (pl.) willing to listen to me and to follow me?
11. That ruler himself had great wealth. (Express in two ways.)
12. You (sg.) stopped and deliberated.

Drill B

Give synopses of the following verbs in the active and middle voices, wherever possible:

1. ἀποθνῄσκω in the third person singular
2. χράομαι in the second person singular
3. αἱρέω in the first person plural
4. νικάω in the third person singular

Drill C

Give the following forms in Greek:

1. dative singular of: that soldier, the same youth, the unjust judge, the large sea
2. genitive singular of: this terrible fate, the immortal youth, the young ruler, the unjust accusation
3. accusative plural of: the handsome youths, the beautiful books, the unjust judges, these strangers.

Exercise A

Translate:

1. ὁ γὰρ δεσπότης τοῖς πολίταις παρέξει ἀλήθειαν καὶ τιμὴν καὶ δικαίους νόμους.
2. ἐπειδὴ πολλὰ καὶ κακὰ αὐτοῖς ἐν τῇ νέᾳ χώρᾳ ἐγένετο, οἱ Ἀθηναῖοι ἐπειρῶντο ἐπὶ τὴν θάλατταν πορεύεσθαι.
3. ὑπὸ τοῦ δεσπότου ἐπαιδεύετο ὥστε πολλοὺς αὐτὸν μέμφεσθαι.
4. οἱ δὲ νόμοι οὕτως ἐποιοῦντο ὥστε οἱ νεανίαι οὐχ οἷοί τ᾽ ἦσαν αὐτοῖς πείθεσθαι.
5. ἐτόλμησε κωλῦσαι τὸν δεσπότην ἀποκτεῖναι τοὺς πολίτας παρὰ τοὺς νόμους.

Exercise B

Translate:

1. After death it will be possible for men to see the gods, since they will have immortal life. (Use dative of possessor.)
2. They made the bridge in such a way that the sea could not destroy it.
3. The wine is so bad that even the soldiers do not wish to accept it.
4. Will the general try to advance with his soldiers against his brother?
5. Time will reveal the excellence of that speech.

14. τὸ Ἡφαιστεῖον. The Temple of Hephaestus, fifth century BC, located on the north-west side of the Agora, Athens.

Lesson 21

Masculine and Feminine Consonant Stems of the Third Declension

<u>Masculine and Feminine Consonant Stems of the Third Declension</u>

     The third declension consists primarily of nouns with stems ending in consonants. The stem of each of these nouns is obtained by dropping the ending from the genitive singular (-ος). The dative plural ending (-σι) causes a wide variety of euphonic changes, when it encounters certain mute stops and other classes of consonants, as outlined below. The euphonic changes involving labials, dentals, and palatals are identical to those already learned for the future tense in Lesson 6.

<u>Labials</u>	π β φ	+ σι = ψι
<u>Palatals</u>	κ γ χ	+ σι = ξι
<u>Dentals</u>	τ δ θ	+ σι = σι
<u>Nasal</u>	ν	+ σι = σι
<u>Liquids</u>	λ / ρ	+ σι = λσι / ρσι

Labial stem: ὁ κλώψ, κλωπός
     thief

<u>singular</u>		<u>plural</u>
κλώψ	Nom.	κλῶπ-ες
κλωπ-ός	Gen.	κλωπ-ῶν
κλωπ-ί	Dat.	κλωψί(ν)
κλῶπ-α	Acc.	κλῶπ-ας

Palatal stem: ὁ κῆρυξ, κήρυκος
     herald

<u>singular</u>		<u>plural</u>
κῆρυξ	Nom.	κήρυκ-ες
κήρυκ-ος	Gen	κηρύκ-ων
κήρυκ-ι	Dat.	κήρυξι(ν)
κήρυκ-α	Acc.	κήρυκ-ας

<u>Notes</u>: Nouns of the consonant declension with a <u>monosyllabic nominative singular</u>, like κλώψ immediately above, are accented on the ultima in the genitive and dative singular and plural.

     Nouns like κῆρυξ, κήρυκος or χάρις, χάριτος below, which have a <u>stem</u> with an acute accent on antepenult, move that accent to the penult when the ultima is long, i.e. in the genitive plural. See also ῥήτωρ, ῥήτορος.

Dental stems: ἡ ἀσπίς, ἀσπίδος   ἡ χάρις, χάριτος
        shield   *favor, goodwill*

singular		plural	singular		plural
ἀσπίς	Nom.	ἀσπίδ-ες	χάρις	Nom.	χάριτ-ες
ἀσπίδ-ος	Gen.	ἀσπίδ-ων	χάριτ-ος	Gen.	χαρίτ-ων
ἀσπίδ-ι	Dat.	ἀσπί-σι(ν)	χάριτ-ι	Dat.	χάρι-σι(ν)
ἀσπίδ-α	Acc.	ἀσπίδ-ας	χάρι-ν	Acc.	χάριτ-ας

<u>Notes</u>: Nouns like ἀσπίς, ἀσπίδος, which have a stem with an acute accent on penult, do not move or change their accents.

Nouns like χάρις, χάριτος, which end in an unaccented -ιδ, -ιθ,-ις, or -ιτ in the nominative singular, drop their stem vowel in the accusative singular and take the alternate accusative ending -ν.

Nasal stem: ὁ χειμών, χειμῶνος   Liquid stem: ῥήτωρ, ῥήτορος
        storm; winter   *speaker, orator*

singular		plural	singular		plural
χειμών	Nom.	χειμῶν-ες	ῥήτωρ	Nom.	ῥήτορ-ες
χειμῶν-ος	Gen.	χειμών-ων	ῥήτορ-ος	Gen.	ῥητόρ-ων
χειμῶν-ι	Dat.	χειμῶ-σι(ν)	ῥήτορ-ι	Dat.	ῥήτορ-σι(ν)
χειμῶν-α	Acc.	χειμῶν-ας	ῥήτορ-α	Acc.	ῥήτορ-ας

<u>Note</u>: Nouns like χειμών, χειμῶνος, which have a stem with a circumflex over a long penult, change that accent to an acute when the ultima is long, i.e. in the genitive plural.

<u>Compensatory Lengthening</u>

If a third declension noun has a stem that ends in two consonants, such as -ντ-, both of which are lost according to the rules governing euphonic change in the chart on the facing page, the noun "compensates" for the loss of letters and thus quantity by lengthening the vowel immediately before the stem as follows:

αντ + σι = ᾱσι
εντ + σι = εισι
οντ + σι = ουσι (see γέρουσι(ν), the dat. pl. of γέρων, γέροντος *old man*)

Vocabulary

ἀσπίς, ἀσπίδος, ἡ *shield*

γέρων, γέροντος, ὁ *old man*
(gerontology)

γυνή, γυναικός, ἡ *woman, wife*
(gynecology)

Ἕλλην, Ἕλληνος, ὁ
(*a*) *Greek* (Hellenism)

κῆρυξ, κήρυκος, ὁ *herald*

κλώψ, κλωπός, ὁ *thief*

πατρίς, πατρίδος,ἡ *fatherland,
country* (patriotic)

ῥήτωρ, ῥήτορος, ὁ *speaker,
orator* (rhetoric)

χάρις, χάριτος, ἡ *favor,
goodwill* (charisma, charity)

χειμών, χειμῶνος, ὁ *storm;
winter*

χάριν ἔχειν (+ dative) *thank,
give thanks (to), feel grateful*

Drill A

Give the following forms; translate:

1. dative plural of:
ὁ γέρων, ἡ ὁδός, ἡ πατρίς, ὁ νεανίας, ὁ κλώψ, ὁ χειμών

2. accusative singular of:
ὁ κῆρυξ, ὁ δεσπότης, ἡ γυνή, ὁ κατήγορος, ἡ χάρις, ἡ πατρίς

3. accusative plural of:
ὁ Ἕλλην, ὁ πόλεμος, τὸ παιδίον, ἡ γυνή, ἡ μοῖρα, ὁ κλώψ

4. nominative plural of:
ἡ ἀσπίς, ὁ ῥήτωρ, ὁ στρατιώτης, τὸ βιβλίον, ὁ χειμών, ἡ χάρις

Drill B

Give the following forms; translate:

1. μέγας to agree with:
χάριν, ἀσπίσι, μοίρας (gen.), γυναῖκες
2. καλός to agree with:
πατρίδι, γυναῖκα, γέροντος, δικασταῖς
3. πολύς to agree with:
κήρυξιν, κλῶπες, χάριτος, πλοῦτος

Drill C

Supply the correct form of the noun to agree with its article:

1. τοῦ (herald)
2. οἱ (old men)
3. τῷ (storm)
4. τὰς (women)
5. τοῖς (thieves)

6. ὁ (speaker)
7. τῆς (shield)
8. τῶν (winters)
9. τοὺς (Greeks)
10. τῇ (goodwill)

Exercise A

Translate:

1. οἱ δὲ Ἕλληνες ἐγένοντο δεσπόται τῆς θαλάττης ὥστε αὐτῆς ἦρχον ἐπ᾽ εἰρήνης τε καὶ πολέμου.
2. ὁ κῆρυξ ὑπέσχετο τοὺς Ἕλληνας χρυσίῳ πείσειν.
3. τοῖς Ἀθηναίοις χάριν ἕξει, τῆς γὰρ πατρίδος αὐτοῦ ἐφείσαντο.
4. εἰ δὲ μὴ ἐχρήσατο τῇ ἀσπίδι, ἀπέθανεν ἂν ὑπὸ τῶν γυναικῶν.
5. οἵδε οἱ ῥήτορές εἰσι δεινοὶ λέγειν, ἀλλὰ τὴν ἀλήθειαν οὐ λέγουσιν.

Exercise B

Translate:

1. The thief deceived us when he stole our gold.
2. The god made a great shield for the soldier.
3. It is possible for us to see many great storms on the sea.
4. The soldiers tried to seize the women and children and to destroy their houses.
5. Because of (his) jealousy the old man killed his wife and fled from (his) country.

Lesson 22

Consonant Stem Nouns (continued) and Vowel Stem Nouns
of the Third Declension

Consonant Stem Nouns of the Third Declension (continued)

a. Neuter dental stems (-ατ)

All neuter nouns in Greek have identical nominative and accusative forms within the same number. In addition, neuter nouns of the third declension take an -α ending in the nominative and accusative plural rather than an –ες or -ας. Neuter stems ending in a dental stem (-ατ) undergo the same euphonic change in the dative plural as masculine and feminine dental stems, namely the dental drops in the presence of sigma (-ατσι ⟶ -ασι).

τὸ χρῆμα, χρήματος *thing;* (plural) *things, property, money*

singular		plural
χρῆμα	Nom.	χρήματ-α
χρήματ-ος	Gen.	χρημάτ-ων
χρήματ-ι	Dat.	χρήμα-σι(ν)
χρῆμα	Acc.	χρήματ-α

b. Sibilant stems (-εσ), ending in -ης or -ος in the nominative singular

When a case ending is added to a sibilant stem, σ becomes intervocalic and thus drops out. In most forms, the remaining vowel(s) in the ending contract(s) with the ε which is still left in the stem. The resulting euphonic changes are identical to those learned for ε-contract verbs (see Lesson 17), with the following additions:

$$1. \quad ε + ι = ει$$
$$2. \quad ε + α = η$$

With such contraction, it is often easiest to identify sigma stem third declension nouns by their nominative singular forms. Neuter sibilant stems end in -ος, like τὸ κέρδος (*gain, profit*) below; masculine and feminine sigma stems end in -ης in the nominative singular, like ἡ τριήρης (*trireme*) below or the proper name ὁ Σωκράτης (*Socrates*). In the charts to follow, the actual form of the noun is written first, followed in parentheses by the uncontracted form.

τὸ κέρδος, κέρδους *gain, profit*

singular		plural
κέρδος	Nom.	κέρδη (κέρδε[σ]α)
κέρδους (κερδε[σ]ος)	Gen.	κερδῶν (κερδέ[σ]ων)
κέρδει (κέρδε[σ]ι)	Dat.	κέρδεσι(ν) (κέρδε[σ]σι)
κέρδος	Acc.	κέρδη (κέρδε[σ]α)

Note: In the dative plural, a σ drops to avoid the redundancy of a second σ.

ἡ τριήρης, τριήρους *trireme*

singular		plural
τριήρης	Nom.	τριήρεις (τριήρε[σ]ες)
τριήρους (τριήρε[σ]ος)	Gen.	τριήρων (τριηρέ[σ]ων)
τριήρει (τριήρε[σ]ι)	Dat.	τριήρεσι(ν) (τριήρε[σ]σι)
τριήρη (τριήρε[σ]α)	Acc.	τριήρεις

Note: The accusative plural τριήρεις is "borrowed" from the nominative plural and hence is irregular.

c. Variable liquid stems -ηρ/-ερ/-ρ(α)

The stems of some liquid stem third declension nouns which end in -ηρ in the nominative singular vary among three grades: strong -ηρ, middle -ερ, and weak -ρ(α). The word ὁ ἀνήρ, ἀνδρός (*man; husband*) shows the weak grade in every form except the nominative (-ηρ) and vocative singular (-ερ) (to be learned later). In contrast, words like ἡ μήτηρ, μητρός (*mother*) below take the middle grade (-ερ) in the accusative and vocative singular, and the nominative, genitive, accusative, and vocative plural. In all variable liquid stems, an α is added in the dative plural (i.e. -ρᾱσι) for euphonic purposes.

ἡ μήτηρ, μητρός *mother*   ὁ ἀνήρ, ἀνδρός *man; husband*

singular		plural	singular		plural
μήτηρ	Nom.	μητέρ-ες	ἀνήρ	Nom.	ἄνδρ-ες
μητρ-ός	Gen.	μητέρ-ων	ἀνδρ-ός	Gen.	ἀνδρ-ῶν
μητρ-ί	Dat.	μητρά-σι(ν)	ἀνδρ-ί	Dat.	ἀνδρά-σι(ν)
μητέρ-α	Acc.	μητέρ-ας	ἄνδρ-α	Acc.	ἄνδρ-ας

Note: The accentuation of μήτηρ and ἀνήρ is irregular.

Vowel Stem Nouns of the Third Declension

a. Variable stems ending in -ευ(ϝ)/-ηυ(ϝ)
b. Variable stems ending in -αυ(ϝ)/-ευ(ϝ)/-ηυ(ϝ)

It is best to memorize the forms of the nouns ὁ βασιλεύς, βασιλέως
(*king*) and ἡ ναῦς, νεώς (*ship*) outright, as the forms or so seemingly irregular,
resulting as they do from complicated euphonic changes. For example, in both
classes of nouns, before another vowel, the υ in the stem shifts to the letter
digamma (ϝ), pronounced like a "w" in English), a letter which was subsequently
eliminated from the Attic dialect. The loss of the digamma, in turn, causes a
process called quantitative metathesis to occur, whereby vowels made adjacent by
contraction exchange quantities. This occurs notably in the genitive singular, where
the long η of the stem is shortened to ε and the short ο of the ending is lengthened
to ω as follows: νηυός → νηϝός → νεώς

ὁ βασιλεύς, βασιλέως *king*   ἡ ναῦς, νεώς *ship*

singular		plural		singular		plural
βασιλεύς	Nom.	βασιλῆς (-εῖς)		ναῦς	Nom.	νῆ-ες
βασιλέως	Gen.	βασιλέ-ων		νεώς	Gen.	νε-ῶν
βασιλε-ῖ	Dat.	βασιλεῦ-σι(ν)		νη-ί	Dat.	ναυ-σί(ν)
βασιλέ-α	Acc.	βασιλέ-ας		ναῦ-ν	Acc.	ναῦς

c. Variable stems ending in -ι/-ει(ϝ)/-ηι(ϝ)

The stem of words like ἡ πόλις, πόλεως (*city*, *city-state*) varies
considerably and is difficult to reconstruct. Like ὁ βασιλεύς and ἡ ναῦς above, it
is best simply to memorize the forms of ἡ πόλις. Briefly, however, ι in the stem
before a vowel became a ϝ, which was subsequently lost, causing further euphonic
change, like the quantitative metathesis that occurs in the genitive singular form:
πόληιος → πόληϝος → πόλεως.

ἡ πόλις, πόλεως *city*, *city-state*   Note: The accents of πόλεως and
                                                            πόλεων are irregular

singular		plural
πόλις	Nom.	πόλεις
πόλεως	Gen.	πόλε-ων
πόλε-ι	Dat.	πόλε-σι(ν)
πόλι-ν	Acc.	πόλεις

Vocabulary

ἀνήρ, ἀνδρός, ὁ *man; husband*
(android)

βασιλεύς, βασιλέως, ὁ *king*
(basilica)

θυγάτηρ, θυγατρός, ἡ *daughter*
(declined like μήτηρ)

κέρδος, κέρδους, τό *gain,*
profit

μήτηρ, μητρός, ἡ *mother*
(matriarchical)

ναῦς, νεώς, ἡ *ship* (nautical)

πατήρ, πατρός, ὁ *father*
(declined like μήτηρ)
(patriarch)

πόλις, πόλεως, ἡ *city, city-state*
(acropolis)

Σωκράτης, Σωκράτους, ὁ
Socrates

τριήρης, τριήρους, ἡ *trireme*

χρῆμα, χρήματος, τό *thing;*
(pl.) *things, property, money*

Drill A

Give the following forms; translate:

1. dative plural of:
   θυγάτηρ, χρῆμα, κέρδος, ναῦς

2. accusative singular of:
   Σωκράτης, ναῦς, πατήρ, Ἕλλην, κέρδος

3. genitive singular of:
   πόλις, ἀνήρ, θυγάτηρ, ναῦς

4. nominative plural of:
   βασιλεύς, πατήρ, πόλις, ναῦς, κέρδος

Drill B

Give the following forms; translate:

1. δίκαιος to agree with:
   ἀνδρῶν, πόλει, βασιλεῦσι, Ἕλληνας

2. ὅδε to agree with:
   Σωκράτους, κέρδη, πολῖται, νεώς

3. ἐκεῖνος to agree with:
   τριήρη, χρῆμα, τριήρεις (acc.), ναῦς (acc.)

Drill C

Change plural forms to singular and vice versa; translate the result:

1. τὰς τριήρεις
2. τῷ βασιλεῖ
3. τοῖς ῥήτορσι
4. τῶν κερδῶν
5. τῇ πατρίδι

6. τῶν νεῶν
7. ὁ ἀνήρ
8. τοῖς χρήμασι
9. τὴν πόλιν
10. τῆς θυγατρός

Drill D

Supply the correct form of the noun to agree with its article:

1. τοῦ (king)
2. τῷ (Socrates)
3. ταῖς (shields)

4. τὰ (things)
5. τοὺς (fathers)
6. ταῖς (ships)

Exercise A

Translate:

1. πολλοί τε καὶ ἄδικοι δικασταὶ τὸν Σωκράτη
ἀπέκτειναν· οὐ γὰρ ἤθελε πείθεσθαι νόμοις ἀδίκους καὶ τὴν
ψυχὴν διαφθείρειν.
2. ταῖς ναυσὶ οἱ Ἕλληνες διὰ τῆς θαλάττης ἐπορεύοντο
καὶ πολλάς τε καὶ καλὰς γυναῖκας ᾖρουν.
3. ὁ γὰρ κλὼψ τὰ χρήματα ἔκλεψεν ἐκ τῆς τριήρους
ὥστε κέρδος μέγα ἐπράξατο.
4. ἐπεὶ ὁ μέγας χειμὼν τὰς τῶν Ἑλλήνων τριήρεις
ἔλυσεν, πολλοὶ ἀπέθανον ἐπὶ θαλάττης καὶ οὐχ οἷοί τ’ ἦσαν
θάπτεσθαι.
5. ἐπειδὴ ὁ ἀνὴρ ἐγένετο ὁ βασιλεὺς καὶ ἡ μήτηρ γυνή.
ἡ πόλις πολλά τε καὶ δεινὰ ἔπασχεν.

Exercise B

Translate:

1. The triremes of the Greeks were fine ships.
2. If we were corrupting the judge, we would be using our
money for the purpose of profit.

Exercise B (continued)

    3. In time of peace sons bury their fathers, but in time of war fathers bury their sons.

    4. When the Greeks came and destroyed the city, many of the king's sons and daughters died.

    5. The king blamed the herald, for he did not prevent the woman from burying her brother.

15. τὰ χρήματα.

Lesson 23

Perfect Active Indicative and Infinitive. Pluperfect Active Indicative

The Perfect Tense

In Greek, the perfect tense expresses a completed act, the consequences of which are represented as having an effect on the present. This tense is often rendered by the English present perfect. Example: πεπαίδευκα, *I have educated.* Greek has two forms of this tense, the first perfect and the second perfect, which differ slightly in formation but usually not in meaning. The perfect active stem is formed from the fourth principal part of the verb.

Reduplication

All forms of the perfect tense receive a spelling change in the stem, called reduplication. This spelling change is part of the fourth principal part, but it can usually be predicted from the first principal part as follows:

a. Verbs with a first principal that begins with a single consonant repeat that consonant and place ε before the stem. Example:

λύω —→ λέλυκα *I have released*

b. Verbs beginning with a mute stop (a labial, palatal, or dental: see Lesson 6) and a liquid (λ, μ, ν, or ρ) reduplicate like verbs beginning with a single consonant. An aspirated mute (φ, χ, or θ), however, is reduplicated without the aspiration, thus φ —→ π, χ —→ κ and, θ —→ τ. Examples:

Mute stop + liquid: κρίνω —→ κέκρικα *I have judged*
Aspirated mute + liquid: χράομαι —→ κέχρημαι *I have used*

c. Verbs beginning with a vowel, double consonant (ζ, ξ, or ψ), or successive consonants other than a mute and a liquid are reduplicated by the use of the augment. Examples:

Vowel: ἀδικέω —→ ἠδίκηκα *I have injured*
Double consonant: ζητέω —→ ἐζήτηκα *I have sought*
Two consonants: σπεύδω —→ ἔσπευκα *I have hastened*

First Perfect Active Indicative and Infinitive

The vast majority of Greek verbs have a first perfect rather than a second perfect. The first perfect is characterized not only by its reduplication but also by the use of κ in the ending. The first perfect active stem consists of the fourth principal part of the verb minus -κα, to which the endings below are added:

singular	person	plural
πε-παίδευ-κα	1	πε-παιδεύ-κα-μεν
I have educated		*We have educated*
πε-παίδευ-κα-ς	2	πε-παιδεύ-κα-τε
You have educated		*You have educated*
πε-παίδευ-κε(ν)	3	πε-παιδεύ-κα-σι(ν)
He/She/It has educated		*They have educated*

Infinitive   πε-παιδευ-κέναι
to have educated

Note: The perfect active infinitive is accented on the penult in spite of its short ultima.

Second Perfect Active Indicative and Infinitive

The second perfect differs in form from the first perfect by the use of a letter other than κ in the ending. Otherwise its conjugation is the same. Examples:

βλάπτω → βέβλαφα *I have harmed*   πράττω → πέπραχα *I have done*
γράφω → γέγραφα *I have written*   τρέπω → τέτροφα *I have turned*
λείπω → λέλοιπα *I have left*

singular	person	plural
λέ-λοι-πα	1	λε-λοί-πα-μεν
I have left		*We have left*
λέ-λοι-πα-ς	2	λε-λοί-πα-τε
You have left		*You have left*
λέ-λοι-πε(ν)	3	λε-λοί-πα-σι(ν)
He/She/It has left		*They have left*

Infinitive   λε-λοι-πέναι
to have left

Pluperfect Active Indicative

The <u>pluperfect</u> tense expresses a past event as having occurred <u>before</u> another past event. It is usually rendered by the English past perfect. Example: ἐπεπαιδεύκη, *I had educated*. The pluperfect stem is formed using the perfect stem, with the following changes:

a. If the perfect active stem begins with a <u>consonant</u>, it is augmented with an ε. Example:

λέλυκα (from λύω) ⟶ ἐλελύκη *I had released*

b. If the perfect stem begins with a <u>vowel</u>, it remains unchanged. Example:

ᾕρηκα (from αἱρέω) ⟶ ᾐρήκη *I had taken*

To complete the conjugation of the pluperfect active, the endings below are added to the stem:

singular	person	plural
ἐ-πε-παιδεύ-κη	1	ἐ-πε-παιδεύ-κε-μεν
I had educated		*We had educated*
ἐ-πε-παιδεύ-κη-ς	2	ἐ-πε-παιδεύ-κε-τε
You had educated		*You had educated*
ἐ-πε-παιδεύ-κει(ν)	3	ἐ-πε-παιδεύ-κε-σαν
He/She/It had educated		*They had educated*

Vocabulary

ἀθροίζω, ἀθροίσω, ἤθροισα, ἤθροικα, ἤθροισμαι, ἠθροίσθην *collect*

ἁρπάζω, ἁρπάσομαι, ἥρπασα, ἥρπακα, ἥρπασμαι, ἡρπάσθην *seize* (Harpies)

βάλλω, βαλῶ, ἔβαλον, βέβληκα, βέβλημαι, ἐβλήθην *throw; hit* (ballistics)

ζητέω, ζητήσω, ἐζήτησα, ἐζήτηκα, ____, ____ *seek, search for*

κρίνω, κρινῶ, ἔκρινα, κέκρικα, κέκριμαι, ἐκρίθην *judge* (crisis)

μένω, μενῶ, ἔμεινα, μεμένηκα, ____, ____ *remain, stay, wait (for)*

παῖς, παιδός, ὁ, ἡ (gen. pl. παίδων) *child, boy, girl* (pediatrics)

πρᾶγμα, πράγματος, τό *deed, act*; (pl.) *trouble* (pragmatic)

δή (postpositive adverb) *in fact, actually*

οὔποτε (μήποτε) *never*

Drill A

Conjugate:

    1. perfect active indicative of: βάλλω
    2. aorist middle indicative of: χράομαι
    3. pluperfect active indicative of: κρίνω

Drill B

Parse and translate the following forms:

1. ἠθροίκασι	6. ἥρπασε
2. ἐμεμενήκη	7. ἥρπακε
3. ἐζητούμεθα	8. ἡρπάκει
4. ἰδεῖν	9. ἑλέσθαι
5. πεπαυκέναι	10. μενοῦσιν

Drill C

Change the form of the verbs as indicated in parentheses; translate the new form:

1. ἐζήτηκε (plural)	5. ἠθελήκασι (pluperfect)
2. ἡρπάκη (plural)	6. μενεῖ (present)
3. ἐκεκρίκης (perfect)	7. λελύκατε (singular)
4. ἐκεκελεύκει (perfect)	8. βεβλήκαμεν (future)

Drill D

Translate:

1. You (pl.) will promise	6. We had released
2. They have written	7. He had injured
3. You (sg.) have done	8. They had trusted
4. I was being stopped	9. We have remained
5. To have guarded	10. To flee (simple aspect)

Exercise A

Translate:

    1.   οἱ δὴ νόμοι Σωκράτη κεκελεύκασι ταύτην τὴν ἀδικίαν κωλύειν καὶ τοὺς κατηγόρους διώκειν.

Exercise A (continued)

2. ἐγὼ γὰρ βεβούλευκα στρατιώτας ἀθροίζειν καὶ
τὰ τῶν συμμάχων χρήματα ἁρπάζειν.
3. εἰ μὴ ὑμεῖς ἤλθετε, ἐπορευόμεθα ἂν ἐπὶ τὸν βασιλέα
ὑμῶν.
4. οἱ δὴ πολῖται ἔβαλον ἂν λίθοις τὸν ῥήτορα, εἰ μὴ ὁ
τοῦ βασιλέως κῆρυξ αὐτοὺς ἔπαυσεν.
5. ἐπὶ τοῦ Σωκράτους πολλοὶ ἀρετὴν ἐκεκρίκεσαν,
ἀλλ᾽ οὔποτε ἐζητήκεσαν αὐτήν.

Exercise B

Translate:

1. If his army had not fled, our women and children would have
remained in the market-place.
2. The Athenians had never harmed guest-friends even in war.
3. Have you (pl.) in fact done this deed?
4. The wise men had educated the children in such a way that
they were actually providing trouble for their fathers and mothers.
5. The Greeks have left us many wise thoughts about
excellence.

16. ὁ θεὸς βαλεῖν μέλλει.

Lesson 24

Perfect Middle-Passive Indicative and Infinitive
Pluperfect Middle-Passive Indicative
Accusative of Respect. Dative of Agent

Perfect Middle-Passive Indicative and Infinitive

The stem for the perfect middle-passive consists of the fifth principal part of the verb minus -μαι. To this stem are added the primary middle-passive personal endings (-μαι, -σαι, -ται, -μεθα, -σθε, -νται); the perfect in Greek is considered to be a primary tense and therefore does not receive an augment. The perfect does <u>not</u> use a thematic vowel between stem and personal ending. The lack of a thematic vowel allows the σ of the second person singular ending -σαι to remain stable.

<u>singular</u>	person	<u>plural</u>
πε-παίδευ-μαι	1	πε-παιδεύ-μεθα
I have educated (for) myself (mid.)		*We have educated (for) ourselves* (mid.)
I have been educated (pass.)		*We have been educated* (pass.)
πε-παίδευ-σαι	2	πε-παίδευ-σθε
You have educated (for) yourself (mid.)		*You have educated (for) yourselves* (mid.)
You have been educated (pass.)		*You have been educated* (pass.)
πε-παίδευ-ται	3	πε-παίδευ-νται
He/She/It has educated (for) him-/her- itself (mid.)		*They have educated (for) themselves* (mid.)
He/She/It has been educated (pass.)		*They have been educated* (pass.)

Infinitive   πε-παιδεῦ-σθαι
to have educated (for) oneself (mid.)
to have been educated (pass.)

<u>Note</u>: As in the active voice, the perfect middle-passive infinitive is accented on the <u>penult</u>.

Pluperfect Middle-Passive Indicative

Like the stem for the pluperfect active, the stem for the pluperfect middle-passive is formed by augmenting (if possible) the perfect middle-passive stem. The <u>secondary</u> middle-passive personal endings, -μην, -σο, -το, -μεθα, σθε, -ντο are added to the verb stem, since the pluperfect <u>is</u> a secondary, that is to say, an augmented tense. As with the perfect middle-passive, no thematic vowel is used between the stem and personal ending.

singular	person	plural
ἐ-πε-παιδεύ-μην	1	ἐ-πε-παιδεύ-μεθα
I had educated (for) myself (mid.)		*We had educated (for) ourselves* (mid.)
I had been educated (pass.)		*We had been educated* (pass.)
ἐ-πε-παίδευ-σο	2	ἐ-πε-παίδευ-σθε
You had educated (for) yourself (mid.)		*You had educated (for) yourselves* (mid.)
You had been educated (pass.)		*You had been educated* (pass.)
ἐ-πε-παίδευ-το	3	ἐ-πε-παίδευ-ντο
He/She/It had educated (for) him-/her-itself (mid.)		*They had educated (for) themselves* (mid.)
He/She/It had been educated (pass.)		*They had been educated* (pass.)

Stem Changes

A verb with a stem ending in a mute consonant undergoes certain spelling changes in the perfect and pluperfect for the sake of euphony. Note that the third person plural of such verbs uses a verbal adjective (perfect participle) in combination with the present indicative of εἰμί to form the <u>perfect</u> tense, and the imperfect indicative of εἰμί to form the <u>pluperfect</u> tense. The endings of the verbal adjective, which are identical to the endings of first and second declension adjective (e.g. πρῶτος, -η, -ον), must agree in gender and number with the subject of the sentence. The verbal adjective is always accented on the <u>penult</u>.

a. Verbs with stems ending in a <u>labial</u> (π, β, φ), including (πτ):

λείπω

Perfect

singular	person	plural
λέλειμμαι	1	λελείμμεθα
λέλειψαι	2	λέλειφθε
λέλειπται	3	λελειμμένοι εἰσί(ν)

Infinitive λελεῖφθαι

Pluperfect

singular	person	plural
ἐλελείμμην	1	ἐλελείμμεθα
ἐλέλειψο	2	ἐλέλειφθε
ἐλέλειπτο	3	λελειμμένοι ἦσαν

b. Verbs with stems ending in a <u>palatal</u> (κ, γ, χ) or (ττ):

ἄγω

Perfect

<u>singular</u>	<u>person</u>	<u>plural</u>
ἦγμαι	1	ἤγμεθα
ἦξαι	2	ἦχθε
ἦκται	3	ἠγμένοι εἰσί(ν)

Infinitive ἦχθαι

Pluperfect

<u>singular</u>	<u>person</u>	<u>plural</u>
ἤγμην	1	ἤγμεθα
ἦξο	2	ἦχθε
ἦκτο	3	ἠγμένοι ἦσαν

c. Verbs with stems ending in a single <u>dental</u> (τ, δ, θ) or otherwise with a 5th principal part ending in -σμαι (but see d, nasals below):

πείθω

Perfect

<u>singular</u>	<u>person</u>	<u>plural</u>
πέπεισμαι	1	πεπείσμεθα
πέπεισαι	2	πέπεισθε
πέπεισται	3	πεπεισμένοι εἰσί(ν)

Infinitive   πεπεῖσθαι

Pluperfect

<u>singular</u>	<u>person</u>	<u>plural</u>
ἐπεπείσμην	1	ἐπεπείσμεθα
ἐπέπεισο	2	ἐπέπεισθε
ἐπέπειστο	3	πεπεισμένοι ἦσαν

d. Verbs with stems ending in a <u>nasal</u> (ν) <u>and</u> 5th principal part in -σμαι:

φαί<u>ν</u>ω

Perfect

<u>singular</u>	<u>person</u>	<u>plural</u>
πέφασμαι	1	πεφάσμεθα
πέφανσαι	2	πέφανθε
πέφανται	3	πεφασμένοι εἰσί(ν)

Infinitive   πεφάνθαι

Pluperfect

<u>singular</u>	<u>person</u>	<u>plural</u>
ἐπεφάσμην	1	ἐπεφάσμεθα
ἐπέφανσο	2	ἐπέφανθε
ἐπέφαντο	3	πεφασμένοι ἦσαν

e. Verbs with present stems ending in a <u>liquid</u> (λ, ρ):

ἀγγέ<u>λλ</u>ω

Perfect

<u>singular</u>	<u>person</u>	<u>plural</u>
ἤγγελμαι	1	ἤγγελμεθα
ἤγγελσαι	2	ἤγγελθε
ἤγγελται	3	ἤγγελμένοι εἰσί(ν)

Infinitive   ἠγγέλθαι

Pluperfect

<u>singular</u>	<u>person</u>	<u>plural</u>
ἠγγέλμην	1	ἠγγέλμεθα
ἤγγελσο	2	ἤγγελθε
ἤγγελτο	3	ἤγγελμένοι ἦσαν

<u>Accusative of Respect</u>

The accusative case without a preposition is used to specify that in respect to which a word or expression is limited. The construction in Greek is somewhat

akin in meaning to the use of the suffix "-wise" in English, as in "skill-wise he is
the best player on the team, but speed-wise he is quite average." Rather than using
a suffix like "-wise" or a phrase like "in respect to," however, Greek simply puts
the limiting word(s) in the accusative case. Examples:

δεινὸς τὸν πόλεμον
terrible in (respect to) war

ὄνομα Σωκράτης
Socrates by (in respect to) name / name-wise, he is Socrates

βέβληται τὸ σῶμα.
He has been struck on (in respect to) his body.

Dative of Agent

The dative case without a preposition is used with the perfect and
pluperfect passive instead of the genitive of agent. Example:

οἱ παῖδες τῇ μητρὶ οὐ βεβλαμμένοι εἰσίν.
The children have not been harmed by their mother.

Vocabulary

ἀφικνέομαι, ἀφίξομαι, ἀφικόμην, _____, ἀφῖγμαι, _____ (with εἰς or
ἐπί + accusative) *arrive (in/at), reach*

ἐπαινέω, ἐπαινέσομαι, ἐπήνεσα, ἐπήνεκα, ἐπήνημαι, ἐπηνέθην *praise,
approve (of)*

θύω, θύσω, ἔθυσα, τέθυκα, τέθυμαι, ἐτύθην *sacrifice*

κτάομαι, κτήσομαι, ἐκτησάμην, _____, κέκτημαι, ἐκτήθην *acquire*

τάττω, τάξω, ἔταξα, τέταχα, τέταγμαι, ἐτάχθην *draw up, station, arrange,
assign* (syntax)

γένος, γένους, τό *race, birth*
(geneology)

σῶμα, σώματος, τό *body*
(psychosomatic)

ὄνομα, ὀνόματος, τό *name,
reputation* (onomatopoeia)

τρόπος, -ου, ὁ *character, way,
manner* (trope)

πεδίον, -ου, τό *plain*

Drill A

Conjugate:

1. perfect middle-passive indicative of: λύω, κρίνω
2. pluperfect middle-passive indicative of: γράφω, παύω

Drill B

Parse and translate the following forms:

1. πέπαυνται
2. ἐλέλυσθε
3. ἔμειναν
4. βαλέσθαι
5. ὄψει

6. ἀφῖξαι
7. ἐπαινοῦμεν
8. τεταγμένοι εἰσί
9. ἐκέκτητο
10. τεθύκατε

Drill C

Change all verbs from the perfect to the pluperfect or vice versa; translate the result:

1. τετόλμηκας
2. ἄφικτο
3. ἐνενικήκειν

4. κέκτημαι
5. ἐτέθυσθε
6. βεβλήκαμεν

Drill D

Change all verbs from the active voice to the middle-passive voice or vice versa; translate the result:

1. σεσωκέναι
2. ἐπήνεσα

3. τεταγμένοι ἦσαν
4. ἠθροίσμην

Exercise A

Translate:

1. Ἕλληνές ἐσμεν τὸ γένος.
2. τῷ δικαστῇ ἐπήνησαι, ἐπεὶ τοὺς τρόπους εἶ δίκαιος.

Exercise A (continued)

3. ἐλέλειπτο δὴ ἐν τῷ πεδίῳ τὸ σῶμα, οὔποτε γὰρ
ἐτέθαπτο τῷ βασιλεῖ ὑμῶν.

4. ἐπειδὴ αἱ τῶν Ἑλλήνων νῆες ἐπὶ τὴν νῆσον
ἀφίκοντο μετὰ τὸν χειμῶνα, ὁ βασιλεὺς τὴν θυγατέρα ἔθυσε
τοῖς θεοῖς.

5. ὄνομα ἄξιον λόγου ἐστὶν ἐκείνῳ τῷ γέροντι, καὶ εἰ
μήποτε τοῖς σοφοῖς πεπαίδευται.

Exercise B

Translate:

    1. A stranger, Socrates by name, has reached our city.

    2. The army had been drawn up in the market-place by the
general.

    3. Some have been honored by the citizens because of (their)
character, others because of (their) judgment.

    4. If he were not so evil in character, he would not dare to steal
your money.

    5. The envy and slander of the many will never harm me, for I
have acquired great wealth.

Lesson 25

Aorist and Future Passive Indicative and Infinitive
Accusative of Duration of Time and Extent of Space

Aorist Passive Indicative

Greek has two forms of the aorist passive, the first and second aorist passive, both of which are formed from the sixth principal part of the verb. The sixth principal part, like the aorist active's third principal part, features a temporal augment. If a verb has a second aorist <u>active</u>, it does not necessarily follow that it will also have a second aorist <u>passive</u>.

First Aorist Passive Indicative and Infinitive

The vast majority of Greek verbs have a first aorist passive rather than a second aorist passive. The first aorist passive is characterized by the tense sign -θη. The stem for the first aorist passive consists of the sixth principal part minus -ν, to which are added the endings below:

singular	person	plural
ἐ-παιδεύ-θη-ν *I was educated*	1	ἐ-παιδεύ-θη-μεν *We were educated*
ἐ-παιδεύ-θη-ς *You were educated*	2	ἐ-παιδεύ-θη-τε *You were educated*
ἐ-παιδεύ-θη *He/She/It was educated*	3	ἐ-παιδεύ-θη-σαν *They were educated*

Infinitive   παιδευ-θῆ-ναι
to be educated

<u>Notes</u>: The infinitive is accented with a circumflex on the penult. As in the aorist active infinitive, the aorist passive infinitive does not take a temporal augment; the infinitive in Greek generally expresses aspect rather than time.

Second Aorist Passive Indicative and Infinitive

The second aorist passive differs in form from the first aorist passive by the replacement of θ with some other letter. Otherwise the conjugation of the first and second aorist passives is identical.

singular	person	plural
ἐ-γρά-φη-ν	1	ἐ-γρά-φη-μεν
I was written (about)		*We were written (about)*
ἐ-γρά-φη-ς	2	ἐ-γρά-φη-τε
You were written (about)		*You were written (about)*
ἐ-γρά-φη	3	ἐ-γρά-φη-σαν
He/She/It was written (about)		*They were written (about)*

Infinitive   γρα-φῆ-ναι
to be written (about)

Future Passive Indicative and Infinitive

The future passive indicative is also formed from the sixth principal part of the verb. It uses the same stem as the aorist passive, minus the augment. The endings for the future passive indicative are identical to those used to form the <u>future middle</u> indicative. A first future passive features a θη; a second future passive replaces θ with another letter.

First Future Passive

singular	person	plural
παιδευ-θή-σομαι	1	παιδευ-θη-σόμεθα
I will be educated		*We will be educated*
παιδευ-θή-σει(-ῃ)	2	παιδευ-θή-σεσθε
You will be educated		*You will be educated*
παιδευ-θή-σεται	3	παιδευ-θή-σονται
He/She/It will be educated		*They will be educated*

Infinitive   παιδευ-θή-σεσθαι
to be about to be educated

Second Future Passive

singular	person	plural
γρα-φή-σομαι	1	γρα-φη-σόμεθα
I will be written (about)		*We will be written (about)*
γρα-φή-σει(-ῃ)	2	γρα-φή-σεσθε
You will be written (about)		*You will be written (about)*
γρα-φή-σεται	3	γρα-φή-σονται
He/She/It will be written (about)		*They will be written (about)*

Infinitive   γρα-φή-σεσθαι
to be about to be written (about)

Middle and Passive Deponents

A deponent verb with a <u>middle aorist</u> is called a <u>middle</u> deponent (example: ἕπομαι, ἕψομαι, <u>ἑσπόμην</u> (*I followed*), ____, ____, ____), and a deponent verb with a <u>passive aorist</u> is called a <u>passive</u> deponent (example: ἥδομαι ἡσθήσομαι, ____, ____, ____, <u>ἥσθην</u> (*I was pleased*)). Certain verbs have both middle and passive forms (example: δέχομαι, δέξομαι, <u>ἐδεξάμην</u> (*I received*), ____, δέδεγμαι, ἐδέχθην (*I was received*)).

Accusative of Duration of Time and Extent of Space

The accusative without a preposition is used in Greek to indicate duration of time or extent of space. These constructions answer the questions "how long?" or "how far?" respectively. Examples:

<u>πολὺν χρόνον</u> ἔμενον.
I waited <u>for a long time</u>.

<u>δέκα στάδια</u> πορεύονται.
They march <u>for ten stades</u>.

Vocabulary

βούλομαι, βουλήσομαι, ____, ____, βεβούλημαι, ἐβουλήθην *want, prefer*

ἥδομαι, ἡσθήσομαι, ____, ____, ____, ἥσθην (+ dative) *be pleased (with)*

ἀπέχω, ἀφέξω (ἀποσχήσω), ἀπέσχον, ____, ____, ____ *keep away;* (+ genitive) *be away from;* (mid.) (+ genitive) *abstain from*

ἔτος, ἔτους, τό *year* (etesian)

ἡμέρα, -ας, ἡ *day* (ephemeral)

στάδιον, -ου, τό *stade* (approx. 600 feet) (stadium)

δέκα (indeclinable adjective) *ten* (decade)

πέντε (indeclinable adjective) *five* (pentagon)

ὅλος, -η, -ον *whole* (holocaust)

μᾶλλον *rather, more*

ἤ (conj.) *or, than*

ἤ ... ἤ *either ... or*

Drill A

Give synopses of the following verbs in the active, middle, and passive voices wherever possible:

1. λύω in the third person singular
2. ἀφικνέομαι in the second person singular
3. λαμβάνω in the first person plural

Drill B

Parse and translate the following forms:

1. ἐβουλήθησαν
2. κατηγόρουν
3. τετρόφατε
4. ᾑρήμεθα
5. λελειμμένοι ἦσαν

6. ἡσθήσει
7. ἀθροισθῆναι
8. πέφασμαι
9. πεπαῦσθαι
10. ἀκηκόασι

Drill C

Change all verbs from the aorist passive to the future passive or vice versa; translate the result.

1. ἐβουλήθην
2. ἐτάχθης
3. ἀχθήσεσθαι

4. ἡσθήσεται
5. σώθησει
6. ἐβουλεύθησαν

Drill D

Change all verbs from the active to the passive voice or vice versa; translate the result.

1. ἐβλάφθη
2. εσφάγημεν
3. πείσεις

4. ἐδιδάξας
5. φανεῖτε
6. λυθησόμεθα

Exercise A

Translate:

1. παρὰ δὴ τῷ βασιλεῖ μενεῖ δέκα ἡμέρας καὶ ὑπ᾽ αὐτοῦ τιμηθήσεται πολλοῖς δώροις.

2. ἐπειδὴ ἡ ἐκείνου τοῦ στρατηγοῦ γυνὴ ὑπὸ τοῦ ξένου ἡρπάσθη, πολλὰ ἔτη οὐκ εἶδεν αὐτήν.

3. οὕτως δὲ ἥσθη τῇ νίκῃ ὁ στρατηγὸς ὥστε πέντε ἡμέρας ἔθυε τοῖς θεοῖς.

4. πολὺν χρόνον ὁ παῖς ἐβούλετο ἢ δεινὸς λέγειν ἢ σοφὸς τὰς γνώμας γίγνεσθαι.

5. τοῖς δὴ Ἕλλησίν ἐστιν ὁ νόμος θάνατον ἑλέσθαι μᾶλλον ἢ ἀδικῆσαι καὶ ὑπὸ τῶν πολιτῶν κριθῆναι.

<u>Exercise B</u>

Translate:

     1. Socrates preferred to die rather than be harmed by his accusers.

     2. I waited until you (sg.) arrived.

     3. It is possible for you (pl.) to stay in Athens for ten days and see the whole city.

     4. The army is said to be ten stades away from the sea.

     5. The Athenians hastened through the city for five stades, for they did not want to be seized by the great king.

17. τὸ στάδιον τὸ ἐν Δελφοῖς.

Lesson 26

Review

Drill A

Give the following forms; translate:

1. pluperfect passive indicative, first person singular of: θάπτω
2. perfect active infinitive of: μένω
3. aorist passive indicative, third person plural of: σφάττω
4. future middle infinitive of: φαίνω
5. future passive indicative, second person singular of: ἥδομαι
6. aorist middle indicative, second person singular of: ἕπομαι
7. imperfect active indicative, third person singular of: ὁράω
8. perfect passive infinitive of: λαμβάνω
9. pluperfect active indicative, third person plural of: πέμπω
10. present middle indicative, second person singular of:
ὑπισχνέομαι

Drill B

Give the following forms:

1. dative singular of:
   παῖς, σῶμα, πεδίον, νεανίας, ἔτος

2. genitive plural of:
   ναῦς, χειμών, χάρις, δεσπότης, κλώψ

3. accusative singular of:
   ἔτος, Σωκράτης, πόλις, ναῦς, ἀνήρ

Exercise A

Translate:

1. τοῦ ἰατροῦ αὐτοῦ κατηγορήκαμεν τήν τε ἀδικίαν καὶ τὴν διαβολήν.

2. ὑπὸ τῆς μητρὸς ἐσφάγησαν οἱ παῖδες, ὁ γὰρ πατὴρ αὐτῶν ἐκείνην ἔψευσεν.

3. ἐπειδὴ τὰ χρήματα εἶδεν, ἀπὸ τιμῆς εἰς κέρδος ἔτρεψε τὰς γνώμας.

Exercise A (continued)

4. ὁ δὲ βασιλεὺς ἥσθη, ἐπεὶ οἱ Ἀθηναῖοι αὐτῷ
χάριν ἔσχον.

5. ἐξέσται ἡμῖν πείθειν τοὺς νεανίας τοῖς πατράσι
πείθεσθαι καὶ χρῆσθαι τοῖς νόμοις;

Exercise B

Translate:

1. I have seen and I have suffered many terrible things at the
hands of the same master.

2. The money would have been stolen from the bank by the
thief, if we had not guarded it.

3. Our city will be saved, for the terrible disease has been
conquered.

4. The father of both men and gods has appeared in the sky.
(use φαίνω in the second perfect active).

5. He wrote the first laws for the Athenians and left the city for
ten years.

18. ἡ ἀσπίς

Lesson 27

Present, Future, and Second Aorist Participles
Attributive Participles. Circumstantial Participles. Future Participle of Purpose

Definition of a Participle

A participle is a <u>verbal adjective</u>. Like an <u>adjective</u>, a participle possesses gender, number, and case, and it can modify or describe a noun or a pronoun; like a <u>verb</u>, it has tense and voice, and it can govern an object or be modified by an adverb or prepositional phrase.

Present Active Participle

In general, the present active participle translates like the "–ing" form of an English verb. Example: παιδεύων *educating*. The specific or idiomatic translation of the participle, however, may differ depending on context or usage, as will be explained in detail in the latter half of this lesson and elsewhere. As such, none of the paradigms below will include a translation of the participle.

The masculine and neuter forms of the present active participle have third declension endings. The masculine forms decline like ὁ γέρων, γέροντος (*old man*); the feminine has first declension endings and declines like ἡ θάλαττα, -ης (*sea*). As with adjectives, the accent is persistent.

a. The present active participle of παιδεύω is declined as follows; the present stem is used (i. e. the first principal part minus -ω):

	masculine	singular feminine	neuter
Nom.	παιδεύ-ων	παιδεύ-ουσ-α	παιδεῦ-ον
Gen.	παιδεύ-οντ-ος	παιδευ-ούσ-ης	παιδεύ-οντ-ος
Dat.	παιδεύ-οντ-ι	παιδευ-ούσ-ῃ	παιδεύ-οντ-ι
Acc.	παιδεύ-οντ-α	παιδεύ-ουσ-αν	παιδεῦ-ον

	masculine	plural feminine	neuter
Nom.	παιδεύ-οντ-ες	παιδεύ-ουσ-αι	παιδεύ-οντ-α
Gen.	παιδευ-όντ-ων	παιδευ-ουσ-ῶν	παιδευ-όντ-ων
Dat.	παιδεύ-ου-σι(ν)	παιδευ-ούσ-αις	παιδεύ-ου-σι(ν)
Acc.	παιδεύ-οντ-ας	παιδευ-ούσ-ας	παιδεύ-οντ-α

Note: The feminine forms of the participle, like the nominative masculine singular (παιδεύων) and the dative masculine and neuter plural (παιδεύουσι(ν)), are the result of euphonic change, namely the loss of -ντ- when it encounters σ and subsequent compensatory lengthening. This euphonic change occurs here in the present tense in the active voice and also in the future and aorist tenses of the participle. Example:

$$\text{παιδεύο[ντ]σα} \rightarrow \text{παιδεύο\underline{ο}σα} \rightarrow \text{παιδεύ\underline{ου}σα}$$

b. The present participle of εἰμί resembles in form the endings of παιδεύων, παιδεύουσα, παιδεῦον (except for the accent):

	masculine	singular feminine	neuter
Nom.	ὤν	οὖσ-α	ὄν
Gen.	ὄντ-ος	οὔσ-ης	ὄντ-ος
Dat.	ὄντ-ι	οὔσ-ῃ	ὄντ-ι
Acc.	ὄντ-α	οὖσ-αν	ὄν

	masculine	plural feminine	neuter
Nom.	ὄντ-ες	οὖσ-αι	ὄντ-α
Gen.	ὄντ-ων	οὐσ-ῶν	ὄντ-ων
Dat.	οὖσι(ν)	οὔσ-αις	οὖσι(ν)
Acc.	ὄντ-ας	οὔσ-ας	ὄντ-α

c. The present active participles of contract verbs follow the regular rules for contraction (see Lessons 17 and 19). Examples:

ε-contract, ποιέω:

	masculine	singular feminine	neuter
Nom.	ποι-ῶν (ποιέων)	ποι-οῦσ-α (ποιέουσα)	ποι-οῦν (ποιέον)
Gen.	ποι-οῦντ-ος (ποιέοντος)	ποι-ούσ-ης (ποιεούσης)	ποι-οῦντ-ος (ποιέοντος)

Note: For the full declension of the present active participle of an ε-contract verb, see Appendix I (Declensions, Participles).

α-contract, τιμάω:

	masculine	singular feminine	neuter
Nom.	τιμ-ῶν (τιμάων)	τιμ-ῶσ-α (τιμάουσα)	τιμ-ῶν (τιμάον)
Gen.	τιμ-ῶντ-ος (τιμάοντος)	τιμ-ώσ-ης (τιμαούσης)	τιμ-ῶντ-ος (τιμάοντος)

Note: For the full declension of the present active participle of an α-contract verb, see Appendix I (Declensions, Participles).

Future Active Participle

The future active participle uses the future active stem (i.e. the second principal part minus -ω). It uses the same endings as the present participle. Examples:

Regular ω-verb, παιδεύω:

	masculine	singular feminine	neuter
Nom.	παιδεύσ-ων	παιδεύσ-ουσ-α	παιδεύσ-ον
Gen.	παιδεύσ-οντ-ος	παιδευσ-ούσ-ης	παιδεύσ-οντ-ος

Liquid future, φαίνω:

	masculine	singular feminine	neuter
Nom.	φαν-ῶν (φανέ[σ]ων)	φαν-οῦσ-α (φανέ[σ]ουσα)	φαν-οῦν (φανέ[σ]ον)
Gen.	φαν-οῦντ-ος (φανέ[σ]οντος)	φαν-ούσ-ης (φανε[σ]ούσης)	φαν-οῦντ-ος (φανέ[σ]οντος)

Second Aorist Active Participle

The second aorist active participle uses the second aorist active stem (i.e. the third principal part of the verb minus -ον) without the temporal augment. Example:

Second aorist, λείπω:

	masculine	singular feminine	neuter
Nom.	λιπ-ών	λιπ-οῦσ-α	λιπ-όν
Gen.	λιπ-όντ-ος	λιπ-ούσ-ης	λιπ-όντ-ος

Present Middle-Passive Participle

Like the present active participle, the present middle-passive participle uses the present stem (i.e. the first principal part minus -ω). The endings -μενος, -μένη, -μενον, which are declined like an adjective of the first and second declensions (see Lesson 9), are added to the stem, with the intervention of the thematic vowel O. In general, the infix -μεν- is the sign for a middle-passive participle in Greek. The only exception to this general rule is the aorist passive participle (see Lesson 28). All middle-passive participles are fully declined in Appendix 1, Declensions, Participles. Examples:

Regular ω-verb, παιδεύω:

	masculine	singular feminine	neuter
Nom.	παιδευ-ό-μεν-ος	παιδευ-ο-μέν-η	παιδευ-ό-μεν-ον
Gen.	παιδευ-ο-μέν-ου	παιδευ-ο-μέν-ης	παιδευ-ο-μέν-ου

ε-contract, ποιέω:

	masculine	singular feminine	neuter
Nom.	ποι-ού-μεν-ος (ποιεόμενος)	ποι-ου-μέν-η (ποιεομένη)	ποι-ού-μεν-ον (ποιεόμενον)
Gen.	ποι-ου-μέν-ου (ποιεομένου)	ποι-ου-μέν-ης (ποιεομένης)	ποι-ου-μέν-ου (ποιεομένου)

α-contract, τιμάω:

	masculine	singular feminine	neuter
Nom.	τιμ-ώ-μεν-ος (τιμαόμενος)	τιμ-ω-μέν-η (τιμαομένη)	τιμ-ώ-μεν-ον (τιμαόμενον)
Gen.	τιμ-ω-μέν-ου (τιμαομένου)	τιμ-ω-μέν-ης (τιμαομένης)	τιμ-ω-μέν-ου (τιμαομένου)

<u>Future and Second Aorist Middle Participles</u>

These participles have the same endings as the <u>present middle-passive</u> participle. The <u>future middle</u> participle uses the future stem (i.e. the second principal part minus -ω). The <u>second</u> aorist middle participle uses the second aorist stem (i.e. the third principal part minus -ον), without the augment. Both participles use the thematic vowel ο between stem and ending. Examples:

<u>Future Middle Participle</u>

Regular ω-verb, παιδεύω:

	masculine	singular feminine	neuter
Nom.	παιδευσ-ό-μεν-ος	παιδευσ-ο-μέν-η	παιδευσ-ό-μεν-ον
Gen.	παιδευσ-ο-μέν-ου	παιδευσ-ο-μέν-ης	παιδευσ-ο-μέν-ου

Liquid future, φαίνω:

	masculine	singular feminine	neuter
Nom.	φαν-ού-μεν-ος (φανε[σ]όμενος)	φαν-ου-μέν-η (φανε[σ]ομένη)	φαν-ού-μεν-ον (φανε[σ]όμενον)
Gen.	φαν-ου-μέν-ου (φανε[σ]ομένου)	φαν-ου-μέν-ης (φανε[σ]ομένης)	φαν-ου-μέν-ου (φανε[σ]ομένου)

<u>Second Aorist Middle Participle</u>

	masculine	singular feminine	neuter
Nom.	λιπ-ό-μεν-ος	λιπ-ο-μέν-η	λιπ-ό-μεν-ον
Gen.	λιπ-ο-μέν-ου	λιπ-ο-μέν-ης	λιπ-ο-μέν-ου

<u>Tense of Participles</u>

The tense of a Greek participle is <u>relative</u> to the main verb. The <u>present</u> participle represents an action <u>simultaneous</u> with that of the main verb; the <u>aorist</u> participle an action <u>prior</u> to that of the verb; and the <u>future</u> participle an action <u>subsequent</u> to that of the verb. The examples below are translated in a variety of different ways, with the idiomatic translations first, the literal translations last. Since Greek tends to use coordination, while English uses subordination, often it is best when translating a participle to turn it into an entire subordinate clause in English. Specific strategies for dealing with the translation of participles will be treated in this Lesson and Lessons 28-29. Examples:

Present Participle:

τὰ χρήματα <u>κλέπων</u> ἐλήφθη.
<u>While taking</u> the money, he was seized. (temporal clause)
<u>Since he took the money</u>, he was seized. (causal clause)
<u>Taking the money</u>, he was seized.

Aorist Participle:

τὴν οἰκίαν <u>λιπὼν</u> ἐλήφθη
<u>After leaving</u> the house, he was seized. (temporal clause)
<u>After he left</u> the house, he was seized (temporal clause)
<u>Having left</u> the house, he was seized.

Future Participle:

οἱ <u>κωλύσοντες</u> ἡμᾶς πολλοὶ ἔσονται.
There will be many <u>to prevent us</u>.
There will be many <u>who will prevent</u> us. (relative clause)
There will be many <u>about to prevent us</u>.

<u>Attributive Participles</u>

Attributive participles function as adjectives or nouns, and thus appear with an appropriate modifying form of the definite article. They are often best translated as relative clauses. Examples:

ἡ <u>φεύγουσα</u> στρατία
the army <u>who is fleeing</u> (relative clause)
the <u>fleeing</u> army

οἱ τὴν νῆσον <u>λιπόντες</u>
<u>those/ the men/ the ones who left</u> the island (relative clause)
<u>those/ the men/ the ones having left</u> the island

αἱ <u>ἀποθανούμεναι</u> ἐσώθησαν.
<u>Those/ the women/ the ones who were about to die</u> were saved. (relative clause)
<u>Those/ the women/ the ones about to die</u> were saved.

ὁ τὸν κλῶπα <u>ἰδών</u> εἰμ' ἐγώ.
I am <u>the one/ man who saw</u> the thief. (relative clause)

Circumstantial Participles

Used <u>without</u> the definite article, circumstantial participles define the circumstances attending the action expressed by the main verb of the sentence or clause sequence. A circumstantial participle is best rendered into English using a subordinate clause to express such things as <u>purpose</u> (see below), <u>time</u>, <u>cause</u>, <u>concession</u>, <u>condition</u>, or <u>means</u>. (for examples, see Lesson 28).

Future Participle of Purpose

The future participle is regularly used in the predicate position to express the <u>purpose</u> or <u>end</u> of an action. The adverb ὡς is sometimes used with the future participle to express a purpose put forward by the subject of the leading verb, but <u>not</u> by the speaker or writer. It may be translated "(in order) to" or "(so as) to." Example:

ἐκάλει αὐτὸν (ὡς) <u>ἐπαινεσόμενος</u>.
He summoned him (in order/ so as) <u>to praise</u> him.

Vocabulary

ἀγγέλλω, ἀγγελῶ, ἤγγειλα, ἤγγελκα, ἤγγελμαι, ἠγγέλθην *announce, report* (angel)

αἰτέω, αἰτήσω, ἤτησα, ____, ᾔτημαι, ____ *ask (for), demand*

καλέω, καλῶ, ἐκάλεσα, κέκληκα, κέκλημαι, ἐκλήθην *call, summon; (pass.) be called* (often with two nominatives)

πάρειμι, παρέσομαι *be present*

ἄρχων, ἄρχοντος, ὁ *ruler*

ἐχθρός, -οῦ, ὁ *(personal) enemy*

τέλος, τέλους, τό *end, result, outcome; (as an adverb, in the accusative singular) finally, at last* (teleology)

ἐχθρός, -ά, -όν *hostile*

πρός (+ genitive) *in the presence of, in the sight of, in the name of, on the side of, like* (characteristic of); *by* (agency)
    (+ dative) *near; in addition to*
    (+ accusative) *to, towards; with regard to; against*

ὡς (+ future participle) *in order (to), so as (to)*

Drill A

Write out the nominative singular in all genders of the present, future, and second aorist participles. Use both the active and middle voices wherever possible:

1. λείπω
2. βάλλω
3. ὁράω

4. ἕπομαι
5. ὑπισχνέομαι
6. αἱρέω

Drill B

Give the following forms:

1. present active participle, dative masculine plural of:
λέγω, αἰτέω, τιμάω, καλέω

2. second aorist active participle, accusative feminine plural of:
λαμβάνω, ἔχω, ὁράω, ἔρχομαι

3. future middle participle, dative neuter singular of:
ἀφικνέομαι, ἀποθνῄσκω, πάσχω, κτάομαι

4. future active participle, accusative neuter singular of:
ἀθροίζω, κρίνω, φυλάττω, ἀγγέλλω

Drill C

Translate the underlined English words or phrases into Greek participles. Make the participle agree in gender, number, and case with the italicized word(s).

1. Seeking an end to his troubles, *Odysseus* landed on Calypso's isle.
2. The soldiers did not heed the orders *of the general* who had chosen to climb the most difficult mountain.
3. The citizens gave thanks *to the men* who were marching into the city.
4. In order to obey their father, *the children* listened carefully.
5. The Thebans did not welcome back kindly *those men* who had fled the enemy in battle.
6. *Men* who are about to speak in the agora practice for many hours.
7. We do not trust *the women* who are blaming each other.
8. Having followed the quarry, *the hunters* were now lost deep in the woods.

Exercise A

Translate:

1. τῷ δὲ πατρὶ ἐπείσατο καὶ ἔλαβε τὸν ἐχθρὸν ὡς ἀποκτενῶν.

2. ἦν πρὸς Σωκράτους μήποτε ἀδικῆσαι καὶ τοὺς ἐχθρούς.

3. ἡμῖν δ' ἦν νόμος πιστεύειν τῷ τὴν ἀλήθειαν λέγοντι.

4. πρὸς δὲ τούτοις εἰ ἤσθημεν τοῖς παροῦσι πράγμασιν, οἱ ἄρχοντες οὐκ ἐκλήθησαν ἂν εἰς τὴν δίκην.

5. οἱ μὲν μεμφόμενοί με φίλοι οὔποτε κληθήσονται, οἱ δ' ἐπαινοῦντες μ' ἐχθροὶ οὔποτε κληθήσονται.

Exercise B

Translate:

1. At last he ordered the ones who were doing these things to stop in the name of the gods.

2. The herald has been sent to announce the outcome of the war to the dying Athenians.

3. The old man came towards us to ask for his son's body in the name of the gods and of men.

4. He used many arguments (= words) in order to persuade the king to sacrifice his daughter.

5. The rulers intended to seize and slay the fugitive.

19. Pericles, the leading statesman in Athens during its "Golden Age" (461 to 429 BC), the era between the Persian and Peloponnesian Wars.

Lesson 28

First Aorist Participles. Circumstantial Participles (continued)

First Aorist Active Participle

The first aorist active participle is formed from the first aorist stem (i.e. the <u>third</u> principal part of the verb minus -σα) without the temporal augment.

First aorist, παιδεύω:

	masculine	singular feminine	neuter
Nom.	παιδεύ-σας	παιδεύ-σασ-α	παιδεῦ-σαν
Gen.	παιδεύ-σαντ-ος	παιδευ-σάσ-ης	παιδεύ-σαντ-ος
Dat.	παιδεύ-σαντ-ι	παιδευ-σάσ-ῃ	παιδεύ-σαντ-ι
Acc.	παιδεύ-σαντ-α	παιδεύ-σασ-αν	παιδεῦ-σαν

	masculine	plural feminine	neuter
Nom.	παιδεύ-σαντ-ες	παιδεύ-σασ-αι	παιδεύ-σαντ-α
Gen.	παιδευ-σάντ-ων	παιδευ-σασ-ῶν	παιδευ-σάντ-ων
Dat.	παιδεύ-σα-σι(ν)	παιδευ-σάσ-αις	παιδεύ-σα-σι(ν)
Acc.	παιδεύ-σαντ-ας	παιδευ-σάσ-ας	παιδεύ-σαντ-α

<u>Note</u>: As with the present active, future active, and second aorist active participles, the stem of the feminine participles (as well as the nominative masculine singular and the dative masculine and neuter plural) feature a "disappearing" -ντ- due to σ and subsequent compensatory lengthening.

Liquid aorist, φαίνω

	masculine	singular feminine	neuter
Nom.	φήνας	φήνασα	φῆναν
Gen.	φήναντος	φηνάσης	φήναντος

First Aorist Middle Participle

The first aorist middle participle uses the first aorist active stem (i.e. the third principal part minus -σα) without the temporal augment. This participle uses the same endings as the other middle-passive participles studied (-μενος, -μένη, -μενον). Unlike the present middle-passive, future middle, and second aorist middle participle, the first aorist middle participle does not use the thematic vowel o to link stem and ending. Instead, the tense sign -σα is used for regular first aorists and a liquid consonant and -α is used for liquid aorists. Examples:

First aorist, παιδεύω:

	masculine	singular feminine	neuter
Nom.	παιδευ-σά-μεν-ος	παιδευ-σα-μέν-η	παιδευ-σά-μεν-ον
Gen.	παιδευ-σα-μέν-ου	παιδευ-σα-μέν-ης	παιδευ-σα-μέν-ου

Liquid aorist, φαίνω:

	masculine	singular feminine	neuter
Nom.	φη-νά-μεν-ος	φη-να-μέν-η	φη-νά-μεν-ον
Gen.	φη-να-μέν-ου	φη-να-μέν-ης	φη-να-μέν-ου

Aorist Passive Participle

The aorist passive participle is formed from the sixth principal part. To form the stem, the temporal augment is removed from the sixth principal part as is the -ην ending. In contrast to the indicative mood, the aorist passive participle features a degradation of the tense sign -θη to -θε.

First aorist passive, παιδεύω:

	masculine	singular feminine	neuter
Nom.	παιδευθ-είς	παιδευθ-εῖσ-α	παιδευθ-έν
Gen.	παιδευθ-έντ-ος	παιδευθ-είσ-ης	παιδευθ-έντ-ος
Dat.	παιδευθ-έντ-ι	παιδευθ-είσ-η	παιδευθ-έντ-ι
Acc.	παιδευθ-έντ-α	παιδευθ-είσ-αν	παιδευθ-έν

	plural		
Nom.	παιδευθ-έντ-ες	παιδευθ-εῖσ-αι	παιδευθ-έντ-α
Gen.	παιδευθ-έντ-ων	παιδευθ-εις-ῶν	παιδευθ-έντ-ων
Dat.	παιδευθ-εῖ-σι(ν)	παιδευθ-είσ-αις	παιδευθ-εῖ-σι(ν)
Acc.	παιδευθ-έντ-ας	παιδευθ-είσ-ας	παιδευθ-έντ-α

Second aorist passive, φαίνω:

	masculine	singular feminine	neuter
Nom.	φαν-είς	φαν-εῖσ-α	φαν-έν
Gen.	φαν-έντ-ος	φαν-είσ-ης	φαν-έντ-ος

Note: The feminine forms of the participle, like the nominative masculine singular and the dative masculine and neuter plural, are the result of euphonic change, as has been the case with the other participles introduced so far. The -ντ- drops from the stem when it encounters σ and by way of compensatory lengthening, ε becomes ει.

Circumstantial Participles

In addition to purpose (see Lesson 27), circumstantial participle may also be used to express time, cause, concession, condition, or means. Examples:

Time ("while," "when," "after"):

> τοῖς θεοῖς θύων ἀπέθανεν.
> *While sacrificing* to the gods, he died.

> τὸ σῶμα θάψας ἔφυγον.
> *After burying* the body, I fled.

> ὁ βασιλεὺς ἐπήνεσε τὴν στρατιὰν ἐν τῷ πεδίῳ ταχθεῖσαν.
> The king praised the army *after it had been drawn up* on the plain.

Cause ("because," "since"):

> οἱ δικασταὶ ἐφείσαντο τοῦ ῥήτορος ἄτε (ὡς) θανάτου ἀξίου οὐκ ὄντος.
> The jurors spared the orator *since (on the grounds that) he was* not worthy of death

Concession ("although"):

ὁ ἄρχων τῷ κήρυκι <u>καίπερ</u> τὴν ἀλήθειαν <u>λέξαντι</u> οὐκ ἐπίστευσεν.
The ruler did not trust the herald <u>although</u> <u>he had told</u> the truth.

Condition ("if"):

σὲ μὴ <u>ὄντα</u> τὸν ἀδελφόν, ἐτιμωρούμην ἄν.
If you <u>were</u> not my brother, I would punish you.

Means ("by"):

πολλὰ <u>πάσχοντες</u> τὴν πόλιν ἔσωσαν.
<u>By suffering</u> many things, they saved the city.

Vocabulary

δεῖ (imperfect ἔδει), δεήσει, δεήσει, ἐδέησε (+ accusative and infinitive) *it is necessary, must, ought*

εὑρίσκω, εὑρήσω, εὗρον (ηὗρον), εὕρηκα (ηὕρηκα), εὕρημαι, εὑρέθην *find* (eureka)

τιμωρέω, τιμωρήσω, ἐτιμωρησάμην, _____, τετιμώρημαι, ἐτιμωρήθην *avenge;* (mid.) *punish, take vengeance on*

φόνος, -ου, ὁ *murder*

ἄλλος, -η, -ο *other, another;* (with article) *the other;* (pl.) *the others, the rest* (allograph)

πολέμιος, -α, -ον *hostile;* (as a plural noun) οἱ πολέμιοι *the enemy* (polemic)

τῷ ὄντι *in fact, really, actually*

ἅτε (+ participle) *since*

καίπερ (+ participle) *although*

ὡς (+ participle, <u>except</u> future) *on the grounds that, as if*

Drill A

Parse the following participles. (Note: To parse a participle, state in order its tense, voice, case, gender, and number, and give its first principal part.):

1. παρούσης
2. αἱρεθεῖσαν
3. ἀφικομένων
4. φυλάξασι
5. μενοῦσι

6. μένουσι
7. βαλόν
8. πεμφθεῖσαι
9. τρέψοντας
10. ἁρπάσαντες

Drill B

Give the following forms:

1. aorist passive participle, accusative masculine singular of: λαμβάνω
2. future middle participle, dative feminine singular of: κρίνω
3. present active participle, accusative neuter singular of: νικάω
4. aorist active participle, nominative neuter plural of: ἄρχω
5. aorist active participle, dative masculine plural of: ὁράω

Exercise A

Translate:

1. καίπερ ξένος ὤν, ὑπισχνοῦμαι σοι τὸν τῆς θυγατρὸς φόνον τιμωρήσειν.
2. οἱ πολῖται τιμῶσι τὸν στρατηγόν, ἅτε δέκα πόλεις τῶν πολεμίων νικήσαντα.
3. ἰδόντες τὰ ὑπὸ τῶν πολεμίων πραχθέντα, οἱ σύμμαχοί σου ἔφυγον πρὸς τὴν θάλατταν.
4. δεῖ σε τῷ ὄντι βουλόμενον τιμᾶσθαι αὐτὸν ἄλλους τιμᾶν.
5. τὸν ἄνδρα ἀποκτείνασα, αὐτὴ ἀπέθανεν ὑπὸ τοῦ υἱοῦ κελευσθέντος πρὸς τῶν θεῶν τὸν τοῦ πατρὸς φόνον τιμωρεῖν.

Exercise B

Translate (using participles wherever possible):

    1. If you (sg.) do not seek, you (sg.) will never find.
    2. If you (pl.) kill Socrates, the gods will punish you (pl.).
    3. Finally his herald came to announce the things which had happened in the city.
    4. In the name of justice, they accused the old man on the grounds that he was corrupting the youths.
    5. By blaming others, he was able to abstain from trouble and fare well.

20. ὁ τοῦ Σαρπήδοντος θάνατος, depicted on the Euphronios Krater, a wine-mixing vessel, c. 515 BC.

Lesson 29

Perfect Participles. Genitive Absolute
Supplementary Participles

Perfect Active Participle

The perfect active participle uses the perfect active stem (i.e. the <u>fourth</u> principal part of the verb minus -κα, or, in the case of a second perfect, whatever consonant precedes -α). It is declined as follows:

	masculine	singular feminine	neuter
Nom.	πεπαιδευ-κώς	πεπαιδευ-κυῖ-α	πεπαιδευ-κός
Gen.	πεπαιδευ-κότ-ος	πεπαιδευ-κυί-ας	πεπαιδευ-κότ-ος
Dat.	πεπαιδευ-κότ-ι	πεπαιδευ-κυί-ᾳ	πεπαιδευ-κότ-ι
Acc.	πεπαιδευ-κότ-α	πεπαιδευ-κυῖ-αν	πεπαιδευ-κός

	masculine	plural feminine	neuter
Nom.	πεπαιδευ-κότ-ες	πεπαιδευ-κυῖ-αι	πεπαιδευ-κότ-α
Gen.	πεπαιδευ-κότ-ων	πεπαιδευ-κυι-ῶν	πεπαιδευ-κότ-ων
Dat.	πεπαιδευ-κό-σι(ν)	πεπαιδευ-κυί-αις	πεπαιδευ-κό-σι(ν)
Acc.	πεπαιδευ-κότ-ας	πεπαιδευ-κυί-ας	πεπαιδευ-κότ-α

Perfect Middle-Passive Participle

The perfect middle-passive participle uses the perfect middle-passive stem (i.e. the <u>fifth</u> principal part minus -μαι). This participle has the same endings as the present middle-passive participle. It may, however, be distinguished from the present participle by the irregular accent occurring on the <u>penult</u>, even when the <u>ultima</u> is short, the reduplicated stem, and the absence of a thematic vowel. Example:

	masculine	singular feminine	neuter
Nom.	πεπαιδευ-μέν-ος	πεπαιδευ-μέν-ος	πεπαιδευ-μέν-ον
Gen.	πεπαιδευ-μέν-ου	πεπαιδευ-μέν-ης	πεπαιδευ-μέν-ου

Genitive Absolute

If a circumstantial participle agrees with a noun or pronoun which shows no grammatical relationship to the main clause of the sentence, both the noun (or pronoun) and the participle are placed in the genitive case to form a genitive absolute. This construction can be used to express the various subordinate ideas described in Lesson 28 in connection with the circumstantial participle, namely time, cause, concession, condition, or means. Example:

ἐμοῦ παρόντος, Σωκράτους κατηγόρει.
In my presence (lit., with me present), he accused Socrates.

Supplementary Participles

A participle that is used to complete the meaning of a verb is called a supplementary participle. It is used with certain Greek verbs (especially λανθάνω and τυγχάνω) in agreement with either the subject or object. Examples:

τὸν γέροντα ἑώρων ἀποθνῄσκοντα.
I saw the old man dying.

ἔτυχεν ἰδὼν τὸν κλῶπα.
By chance he saw the thief. (lit., *he happened having seen / to see the thief.*)

τὸν πατέρα ἐλάνθανεν ὁ παῖς τὰ χρήματα αἰτῶν.
The child asked for the money without the knowledge of his father.
(lit., *The child asking for the money escaped the notice of his father*)

Note: The action expressed by the supplementary particle in Greek is often best rendered in English as the main verb of the sentence, whereas the main verb in Greek is often best rendered by an English adverb or prepositional phrase.

Vocabulary

δέομαι, δεήσομαι, ____, ____, ____, ἐδεήθην (+ genitive) *ask; need*

ἐπιβουλεύω, ἐπιβουλεύσω, ἐπεβούλευσα, ἐπιβεβούλευκα,
    ἐπιβεβούλευμαι, ἐπεβουλεύθην (+ dative) *plot against*

συμβουλεύω, συμβουλεύσω, συνεβούλευσα, συμβεβούλευκα,
    συμβεβούλευμαι, συνεβουλεύθην (+ dative) *advise*; (mid.) *consult (with),*
    ask the advice of

λανθάνω, λήσω, ἔλαθον, λέληθα, λέλησμαι, ____ (+ suppl. participle)
    escape the notice of

ἐπιλανθάνομαι, ἐπιλήσομαι, ἐπελαθόμην, ____, ἐπιλέλησμαι, ____
(+ genitive) *forget*

τυγχάνω, τεύξομαι, ἔτυχον, τετύχηκα, ____, ____ (+ suppl. participle)
happen; (+ genitive) *gain, hit, meet*

παρασκευάζω, παρασκευάσω, παρεσκεύασα, παρεσκεύακα,
παρεσκεύασμαι, παρεσκευάσθην *prepare;* (mid.) *make preparations*

πλέω, πλεύσομαι, ἔπλευσα, πέπλευκα, πέπλευσμαι, ____ *sail*

γῆ, γῆς, ἡ *earth, land, ground, country* (geology)

ἐνταῦθα (adverb) *there, in that place, to that place; here; then*

κατά (+ genitive) *down from, down under; against* (e.g. καθ᾽ ἡμῶν ἔλεξεν, *he
              spoke against us*)
   (+ acc.) *down along* (e.g. κατὰ γῆν καὶ κατὰ θάλατταν, *by land and by
              sea*); *throughout; according to; opposite; by* (distributively, e.g. , καθ᾽
              ἡμέραν, *day by day*)

Note: δέομαι and πλέω <u>do not contract</u> in the present and imperfect when ε is
followed by ο or ω, e.g. πλέουσι, ἔπλεον; δεόμεθα, ἐδεόμην.

Drill A

Translate:

1. παῖδες δ᾽ ἦμεν τῆς μητρὸς ἀποθανούσης.
2. τὰ χρήματα ἐλάνθανε δεχόμενος.
3. οὐ πιστεύω τοῖς πολλὰ ὑπισχνουμένοις.
4. ὑμᾶς δεῖ τὴν ἀσπίδα εὑρεῖν.
5. αἱ τῶν τεθνηκότων ψυχαὶ κατὰ τῆς γῆς ἔρχονται.
6. ὁ χειμὼν τὰς ναῦς ἐκώλυε μὴ πλεῖν.

Drill B

Translate:

1. I heard him speaking.
2. He happens to be faring well.
3. According to you he lied, but according to me he forgot.
4. The orator wrote a speech against Socrates.
5. The king advanced to punish the enemy.
6. A storm stopped our triremes from sailing.

<u>Exercise A</u>

Translate:

1. ὁ δὴ θεὸς ἐλθὼν κατ' οὐρανοῦ ἐτύγχανε καὶ ἐπὶ γῆς πολλὰ ἔτη μένων.

2. ἡ γυνὴ ἐπιβουλεύουσα τῇ θυγατρὶ τὸν βασιλέα ἐλάνθανεν.

3. οἱ Ἕλληνες κατὰ γῆν καὶ κατὰ θάλατταν πορευθέντες ἐπὶ τὸν ποταμὸν ἔπλεον καὶ περὶ τὴν πολεμίων νῆσον.

4. καθ' ἡμέραν οἱ ξένοι ἠδικημένοι κατηγορίαις τε καὶ διαβολῇ εἰς τὴν ἀγορὰν ἦλθον ὡς τὴν δίκην αἰτήσοντες.

5. τῶν πολεμίων ἐνταῦθα παρόντων, οἱ στρατιῶται ἤρξαντο τρέπεσθαι καὶ φεύγειν.

<u>Exercise B</u>

Translate (using participles wherever possible):

1. He actually happened to be present when Socrates was dying.
2. The judge was making preparations to hear the orators.
3. I have advised him to write another book about the earth.
4. Since the ruler is dead (has died), the whole city is faring badly.
5. Then he asked me to consult Socrates about our expedition.

21. ἡ κλεψύδρα. Water-clock, used for limiting the time allotted for speeches in the Athenian court.

Lesson 30

Review

Exercise A: Reading

The selection below has been adapted from the *Histories* of Herodotus, often called
the "Father of History." Herodotus was born in the city of Halicarnassus, situated
in southwest Asia Minor (modern day Turkey), about 484 BC. His birth probably
occurred during the decade when Greece was being threatened by the Persians–
first under Darius in 490 BC and then under his son Xerxes ten years later. The era
of his birth probably influenced Herodotus to write of the momentous conflict
between East and West, which he employed as the central theme for his *Histories*.
Herodotus was one of the first Greek historians to organize his material, derived
from legends, hearsay, chronological writings, and personal observations through
extensive travels, into a unified work. He is considered one of the earliest
formative influences in the development of classical Greek prose. The following
episodes describe Darius' unsuccessful invasion of Scythia, undertaken in 512 BC
to punish the Scythians who had previously invaded part of his own great empire.

The expedition begins. Darius grants a request.

Παρασκευαζομένου Δαρείου ἐπὶ τοὺς Σκύθας καὶ
περιπέμποντος κήρυκας κελεύσοντας τοὺς μὲν στρατιάν, τοὺς δὲ
γέφυραν ποιεῖν διὰ τοῦ Βοσπόρου, Ἀρτάβανος ὁ Ὑστάσπους,
ἀδελφὸς ὢν Δαρείου, ἐπειρᾶτο πείθειν αὐτὸν μὴ στρατιὰν ἐπὶ
5   Σκύθας ποιεῖσθαι, λέγων τοὺς ἐν τοῖς Σκύθαις κινδύνους. ἀλλ'
οὐ γὰρ ἔπειθε καίπερ εὖ συμβουλεύων αὐτῷ, ὁ μὲν ἐπέπαυτο, ὁ δέ,
ἐπειδὴ αὐτῷ ταῦτα παρεσκεύαστο, ἐξήγαγε τὴν στρατιὰν ἐκ Σούσων.
ἐνταῦθα Οἰόβαζος, γένος μὲν Πέρσης, ἐδεήθη Δαρείου, τριῶν
ὄντων αὐτῷ παίδων, ἕνα αὐτῷ καταλειφθῆναι.
10   Ὁ δὲ ἔλεξε τάδε· ὡς φίλῳ ὄντι καὶ δικαίων δεομένῳ σοι
πάντας τοὺς παῖδας καταλείψω.
Ὁ μὲν δὴ Οἰόβαζος ἤσθη, ὡς τῶν υἱῶν ἀπὸ στρατιᾶς
λελυμένων, ὁ δὲ ἐκέλευσε τοὺς στρατηγοὺς ἀποκτεῖναι τοὺς
Οἰοβάζου παῖδας. καὶ οὗτοι μὲν ἀποσφαγέντες ἐνταῦθα ἐλείποντο.

Adapted from Herodotus, *Histories* 4.83-84

1   Δαρείου from Δαρεῖος, -ου, ὁ *Darius* (king of Persia)
Σκύθας from Σκύθαι, -ῶν, οἱ *Scythians* (a nomadic people inhabiting vast
areas east of the Danube river)

3   Βοσπόρου from Βόσπορος, -ου, ὁ *Bosporus* (a strait connecting the Black
    Sea with the Sea of Marmora and the eastern Mediterranean Sea)
    Ἀρτάβανος, -ου, ὁ *Artabanus* (governor of Parthia)
    ὁ supply υἱός
    Ὑστάσπους, from Ὑστάσπης, -ους, ὁ *Hystaspes* (father of Darius
    and Artabanus)

6   γάρ here meaning *since*

7   Σούσων from Σοῦσα, -ων, τά *Susa* (Persian capital; site of the chief royal
    palace)

8   Οἰόβαζος, -ου, ὁ *Oeobazus* (a Persian noble)
    Πέρσης, -ου, ὁ *a Persian*
    τριῶν genitive plural of τρεῖς, τρία *three*

9   παίδων here = υἱῶν. The sons of Oeobazus were to serve in the expedition
    against the Scythians.
    ἕνα accusative of εἷς, ἑνός *one*, subject of the infinitive καταλειφθῆναι;
    translate: *that one be left behind for him*

11 πάντας accusative plural of πᾶς, πᾶσα, πᾶν *all*

<u>Exercise B</u>

Translate:

     1. In order to gain victory, you must have money in addition to
virtue.

     2. The soldiers were ordered to punish the strangers day by day
although they had not done wrong.

     3. The Greeks made a great horse and stationed soldiers there
without the knowledge of the enemy.

     4. In the name of the gods we asked the ruler to spare the rest
on the grounds that they were Athenians by birth.

     5. Pursued by a terrible enemy, the young man fled around the
city and suffered an evil fate in the presence of his friends.

22. ὁ Ἡρόδοτος

Declensions

Declensions

The Definite Article

	Masculine	Feminine	Neuter
		Singular	
Nominative	ὁ	ἡ	τό
Genitive	τοῦ	τῆς	τοῦ
Dative	τῷ	τῇ	τῷ
Accusative	τόν	τήν	τό

		Plural	
Nominative	οἱ	αἱ	τά
Genitive	τῶν	τῶν	τῶν
Dative	τοῖς	ταῖς	τοῖς
Accusative	τούς	τάς	τά

Nouns

The First Declension

Category	1a(Fem.)	b(Fem.)	2a(Fem.)	b(Fem.)	3a(Masc.)	b(Masc.)
			Singular			
Nom.	ἀρετή	οἰκία	θάλαττα	μοῖρα	πολίτης	νεανίας
Gen.	ἀρετῆς	οἰκίας	θαλάττης	μοίρας	πολίτου	νεανίου
Dat.	ἀρετῇ	οἰκίᾳ	θαλάττῃ	μοίρᾳ	πολίτῃ	νεανίᾳ
Acc.	ἀρετήν	οἰκίαν	θάλατταν	μοῖραν	πολίτην	νεανίαν

			Plural			
Nom.	ἀρεταί	οἰκίαι	θάλατται	μοῖρα	πολῖται	νεανίαι
Gen.	ἀρετῶν	οἰκιῶν	θαλαττῶν	μοιρῶν	πολιτῶν	νεανιῶν
Dat.	ἀρεταῖς	οἰκίαις	θαλάτταις	μοίραις	πολίταις	νεανίαις
Acc.	ἀρετάς	οἰκίας	θαλάττας	μοίρας	πολίτας	νεανίας

The Second Declension

	Masculine	Feminine	Neuter
		Singular	
Nom.	ἄνθρωπος	ὁδός	παιδίον
Gen.	ἀνθρώπου	ὁδοῦ	παιδίου
Dat.	ἀνθρώπῳ	ὁδῷ	παιδίῳ
Acc.	ἄνθρωπον	ὁδόν	παιδίον

Declensions

	Plural		
Nom.	ἄνθρωποι	ὁδοί	παιδία
Gen.	ἀνθρώπων	ὁδῶν	παιδίων
Dat.	ἀνθρώποις	ὁδοῖς	παιδίοις
Acc.	ἀνθρώπους	ὁδούς	παιδία

The Third Declension

Masculine & Feminine Consonant Stems

Singular

	Labial (-π,-β,-φ)	Palatal (-κ,-γ,-ξ)	Dental (-τ,-δ,-θ)	Nasal (-ων)
Nom.	κλώψ	κῆρυξ	ἀσπίς	χειμών
Gen.	κλωπός	κήρυκος	ἀσπίδος	χειμῶνος
Dat.	κλωπί	κήρυκι	ἀσπίδι	χειμῶνι
Acc.	κλῶπα	κήρυκα	ἀσπίδα	χειμῶνα

Plural

Nom.	κλῶπες	κήρυκες	ἀσπίδες	χειμῶνες
Gen.	κλωπῶν	κηρύκων	ἀσπίδων	χειμώνων
Dat.	κλωψί(ν)	κήρυξι(ν)	ἀσπίσι(ν)	χειμῶσι(ν)
Acc.	κλῶπας	κήρυκας	ἀσπίδας	χειμῶνας

Singular

	Nasal/Dental (-οντ)	Sibilant (-εσ)	Liquid (-ρ)	(-ηρ/-ερ/-ρ(α))	
Nom.	γέρων	τριήρης	ῥήτωρ	μήτηρ	ἀνήρ
Gen.	γέροντος	τριήρους	ῥήτορος	μητρός	ἀνδρός
Dat.	γέροντι	τριήρει	ῥήτορι	μητρί	ἀνδρί
Acc.	γέροντα	τριήρη	ῥήτορα	μητέρα	ἄνδρα

Plural

Nom.	γέροντες	τριήρεις	ῥήτορες	μητέρες	ἄνδρες
Gen.	γερόντων	τριήρων	ῥητόρων	μητέρων	ἀνδρῶν
Dat.	γέρουσι(ν)	τριήρεσι(ν)	ῥήτορσι(ν)	μητράσι(ν)	ἀνδράσι(ν)
Acc.	γέροντας	τριήρεις	ῥήτορας	μητέρας	ἄνδρας

Neuter Consonant Stems

	Sibilant (-εσ)		Dental (-ατ)	
	Singular	Plural	Singular	Plural
Nom.	κέρδος	κέρδη	χρῆμα	χρήματα
Gen.	κέρδους	κερδῶν	χρήματος	χρημάτων
Dat.	κέρδει	κέρδεσι(ν)	χρήματι	χρήμασι(ν)
Acc.	κέρδος	κέρδη	χρῆμα	χρήματα

Declensions

Masculine and Feminine Variable Vowel Stems

Singular

	-ευ(ϝ)/-ηυ(ϝ)	-αυ(ϝ)/-ευ(ϝ)/-ηυ(ϝ)	-ι/-ει(ϝ)/-ηυ(ϝ)
Nom.	βασιλεύς	ναῦς	πόλις
Gen.	βασιλέως	νεώς	πόλεως
Dat.	βασιλεῖ	νηί	πόλει
Acc.	βασιλέα	ναῦν	πόλιν

Plural

Nom.	βασιλῆς (-εῖς)	νῆες	πόλεις
Gen.	βασιλέων	νεῶν	πόλεων
Dat.	βασιλεῦσι(ν)	ναυσί(ν)	πόλεσι(ν)
Acc.	βασιλέας	ναῦς	πόλεις

Adjectives

First and Second Declension

Singular

	Three Terminations			Two Terminations	
	Masculine	Feminine	Neuter	Masc./Fem.	Neuter
Nom.	πρῶτος	πρώτη	πρῶτον	ἄδικος	ἄδικον
Gen.	πρώτου	πρώτης	πρώτου	ἀδίκου	ἀδίκου
Dat.	πρώτῳ	πρώτῃ	πρώτῳ	ἀδίκῳ	ἀδίκῳ
Acc.	πρῶτον	πρώτην	πρῶτον	ἄδικον	ἄδικον

Plural

Nom.	πρῶτοι	πρῶται	πρῶτα	ἄδικοι	ἄδικα
Gen.	πρώτων	πρώτων	πρώτων	ἀδίκων	ἀδίκων
Dat.	πρώτοις	πρώταις	πρώτοις	ἀδίκοις	ἀδίκοις
Acc.	πρώτους	πρώτας	πρῶτα	ἀδίκους	ἄδικα

Irregular First and Second Declension

Singular

	Masculine	Feminine	Neuter	Masculine	Feminine	Neuter
Nom.	μέγας	μεγάλη	μέγα	πολύς	πολλή	πολύ
Gen.	μεγάλου	μεγάλης	μεγάλου	πολλοῦ	πολλῆς	πολλοῦ
Dat.	μεγάλῳ	μεγάλῃ	μεγάλῳ	πολλῷ	πολλῇ	πολλῷ
Acc.	μέγαν	μεγάλην	μέγα	πολύν	πολλήν	πολύ

Declensions

Plural

Nom.	μεγάλοι	μεγάλαι	μεγάλα	πολλοί	πολλαί	πολλά
Gen.	μεγάλων	μεγάλων	μεγάλων	πολλῶν	πολλῶν	πολλῶν
Dat.	μεγάλοις	μεγάλαις	μεγάλοις	πολλοῖς	πολλαῖς	πολλοῖς
Acc.	μεγάλους	μεγάλας	μεγάλα	πολλούς	πολλάς	πολλά

Participles

Present Active (Regular ω-Verbs)
Singular

	Masculine	Feminine	Neuter
Nom.	παιδεύων	παιδεύουσα	παιδεῦον
Gen.	παιδεύοντος	παιδευούσης	παιδεύοντος
Dat.	παιδεύοντι	παιδευούσῃ	παιδεύοντι
Acc.	παιδεύοντα	παιδεύουσαν	παιδεῦον

Plural

	Masculine	Feminine	Neuter
Nom.	παιδεύοντες	παιδεύουσαι	παιδεύοντα
Gen.	παιδευόντων	παυδευουσῶν	παιδευόντων
Dat.	παιδεύουσι(ν)	παιδευούσαις	παιδεύουσι(ν)
Acc.	παιδεύοντας	παιδευούσας	παιδεύοντα

Present Active (ε-contract Verbs)
Singular

	Masculine	Feminine	Neuter
Nom.	ποιῶν	ποιοῦσα	ποιοῦν
Gen.	ποιοῦντος	ποιούσης	ποιοῦντος
Dat.	ποιοῦντι	ποιούσῃ	ποιοῦντι
Acc.	ποιοῦντα	ποιοῦσαν	ποιοῦν

Plural

	Masculine	Feminine	Neuter
Nom.	ποιοῦντες	ποιοῦσαι	ποιοῦντα
Gen.	ποιούντων	ποιουσῶν	ποιούντων
Dat.	ποιοῦουσι(ν)	ποιούσαις	ποιοῦουσι(ν)
Acc.	ποιοῦντας	ποιούσας	ποιοῦντα

Present Active (α-contract Verbs)
Singular

	Masculine	Feminine	Neuter
Nom.	τιμῶν	τιμῶσα	τιμῶν
Gen.	τιμῶντος	τιμώσης	τιμῶντος
Dat.	τιμῶντι	τιμώσῃ	τιμῶντι
Acc.	τιμῶντα	τιμῶσαν	τιμῶν

Declensions

Plural

	Masculine	Feminine	Neuter
Nom.	τιμῶντες	τιμῶσαι	τιμῶντα
Gen.	τιμώντων	τιμωσῶν	τιμώντων
Dat.	τιμῶσι(ν)	τιμώσαις	τιμῶσι(ν)
Acc.	τιμῶντας	τιμώσας	τιμῶντα

Future Active (Regular ω-Verbs)
Singular

	Masculine	Feminine	Neuter
Nom.	παιδεύσων	παιδεύσουσα	παιδεῦσον
Gen.	παιδεύσοντος	παιδευσούσης	παιδεύσοντος
Dat.	παιδεύσοντι	παιδευσούσῃ	παιδεύσοντι
Acc.	παιδεύσοντα	παιδεύσουσαν	παιδεῦσον

Plural

	Masculine	Feminine	Neuter
Nom.	παιδεύσοντες	παιδεύσουσαι	παιδεύσοντα
Gen.	παιδευσόντων	παιδευσουσῶν	παιδευσόντων
Dat.	παιδεύσουσι(ν)	παιδευσούσαις	παιδεύσουσι(ν)
Acc.	παιδεύσοντας	παιδευσούσας	παιδεύσοντα

Future Active (Liquid Verbs)
Singular

	Masculine	Feminine	Neuter
Nom.	φανῶν	φανοῦσα	φανοῦν
Gen.	φανοῦντος	φανούσης	φανοῦντος
Dat.	φανοῦντι	φανούσῃ	φανοῦντι
Acc.	φανοῦντα	φανοῦσαν	φανοῦν

Plural

	Masculine	Feminine	Neuter
Nom.	φανοῦντες	φανοῦσαι	φανοῦντα
Gen.	φανούντων	φανουσῶν	φανούντων
Dat.	φανοῦουσι(ν)	φανούσαις	φανοῦουσι(ν)
Acc.	φανοῦντας	φανούσας	φανοῦντα

First Aorist Active
Singular

	Masculine	Feminine	Neuter
Nom.	παιδεύσας	παιδεύσασα	παιδεῦσαν
Gen.	παιδεύσαντος	παιδευσάσης	παιδεύσαντος
Dat.	παιδεύσαντι	παιδευσάσῃ	παιδεύσαντι
Acc.	παιδεύσαντα	παιδευσάσαν	παιδεῦσαν

Declensions

	Masculine	Plural Feminine	Neuter
Nom.	παιδεύσαντες	παιδεύσασαι	παιδεύσαντα
Gen.	παιδευσάντων	παιδευσασῶν	παιδευσάντων
Dat.	παιδεύσασι(ν)	παιδευσάσαις	παιδεύσασι(ν)
Acc.	παιδεύσαντας	παιδευσάσας	παιδεύσαντα

Second Aorist Active
Singular

	Masculine	Feminine	Neuter
Nom.	λιπών	λιποῦσα	λιπόν
Gen.	λιπόντος	λιπούσης	λιπόντος
Dat.	λιπόντι	λιπούσῃ	λιπόντι
Acc.	λιπόντα	λιποῦσαν	λιπόν

	Masculine	Plural Feminine	Neuter
Nom.	λιπόντες	λιποῦσαι	λιπόντα
Gen.	λιπόντων	λιπουσῶν	λιπόντων
Dat.	λιποῦσι(ν)	λιπούσαις	λιποῦσι(ν)
Acc.	λιπόντας	λιπούσας	λιπόντα

Perfect Active
Singular

	Masculine	Feminine	Neuter
Nom.	πεπαιδευκώς	πεπαιδευκυῖα	πεπαιδευκός
Gen.	πεπαιδευκότος	πεπαιδευκυίας	πεπαιδευκότος
Dat.	πεπαιδευκότι	πεπαιδευκυίᾳ	πεπαιδευκότι
Acc.	πεπαιδευκότα	πεπαιδευκυῖαν	πεπαιδευκός

	Masculine	Plural Feminine	Neuter
Nom.	πεπαιδευκότες	πεπαιδευκυῖαι	πεπαιδευκότα
Gen.	πεπαιδευκότων	πεπαιδευκυιῶν	πεπαιδευκότων
Dat.	πεπαιδευκόσι(ν)	πεπαιδευκυίαις	πεπαιδευκόσι(ν)
Acc.	πεπαιδευκότας	πεπαιδευκυίας	πεπαιδευκότα

Present Middle-Passive (Regular ω-Verbs)
Singular

	Masculine	Feminine	Neuter
Nom.	παιδευόμενος	παιδευομένη	παιδευόμενον
Gen.	παιδευομένου	παιδευομένης	παιδευομένου
Dat.	παιδευομένῳ	παιδευομένῃ	παιδευομένῳ
Acc.	παιδευόμενον	παιδευομένην	παιδευόμενον

Declensions

Nom.	παιδευόμενοι	παιδευόμεναι	παιδευόμενα
Gen.	παιδευομένων	παιδευομένων	παιδευομένων
Dat.	παιδευομένοις	παιδευομέναις	παιδευομένοις
Acc.	παιδευομένους	παιδευομένας	παιδευόμενα

Present Middle-Passive (ε-contract Verbs)
Singular

	Masculine	Feminine	Neuter
Nom.	ποιούμενος	ποιουμένη	ποιούμενον
Gen.	ποιουμένου	ποιουμένης	ποιουμένου
Dat.	ποιουμένῳ	ποιουμένῃ	ποιουμένῳ
Acc.	ποιούμενον	ποιουμένην	ποιούμενον

Plural

Nom.	ποιούμενοι	ποιούμεναι	ποιούμενα
Gen.	ποιουμένων	ποιουμένων	ποιουμένων
Dat.	ποιουμένοις	ποιουμέναις	ποιουμένοις
Acc.	ποιουμένους	ποιουμένας	ποιούμενα

Present Middle-Passive (α-contract Verbs)
Singular

	Masculine	Feminine	Neuter
Nom.	τιμώμενος	τιμωμένη	τιμώμενον
Gen.	τιμωμένου	τιμωμένης	τιμωμένου
Dat.	τιμωμένῳ	τιμωμένῃ	τιμωμένῳ
Acc.	τιμώμενον	τιμωμένην	τιμώμενον

Plural

Nom.	τιμώμενοι	τιμώμεναι	τιμώμενα
Gen.	τιμωμένων	τιμωμένων	τιμωμένων
Dat.	τιμωμένοις	τιμωμέναις	τιμωμένοις
Acc.	τιμωμένους	τιμωμένας	τιμώμενα

Future Middle (Regular ω-Verbs)
Singular

	Masculine	Feminine	Neuter
Nom.	παιδευσόμενος	παιδευσομένη	παιδευσόμενον
Gen.	παιδευσομένου	παιδευσομένης	παιδευσομένου
Dat.	παιδευσομένῳ	παιδευσομένῃ	παιδευσομένῳ
Acc.	παιδευσόμενον	παιδευσομένην	παιδευσόμενον

Declensions

Plural

Nom.	παιδευσόμενοι	παιδευσόμεναι	παιδευσόμενα
Gen.	παιδευσομένων	παιδευσομένων	παιδευσομένων
Dat.	παιδευσομένοις	παιδευσομέναις	παιδευσομένοις
Acc.	παιδευσομένους	παιδευσομένας	παιδευσόμενα

Future Middle (Liquid Verbs)
Singular

	Masculine	Feminine	Neuter
Nom.	φανούμενος	φανουμένη	φανούμενον
Gen.	φανουμένου	φανουμένης	φανουμένου
Dat.	φανουμένῳ	φανουμένῃ	φανουμένῳ
Acc.	φανούμενον	φανουμένην	φανούμενον

Plural

Nom.	φανούμενοι	φανούμεναι	φανούμενα
Gen.	φανουμένων	φανουμένων	φανουμένων
Dat.	φανουμένοις	φανουμέναις	φανουμένοις
Acc.	φανουμένους	φανουμένας	φανούμενα

First Aorist Middle
Singular

	Masculine	Feminine	Neuter
Nom.	παιδευσάμενος	παιδευσαμένη	παιδευσάμενον
Gen.	παιδευσαμένου	παιδευσαμένης	παιδευσαμένου
Dat.	παιδευσαμένῳ	παιδευσαμένῃ	παιδευσαμένῳ
Acc.	παιδευσάμενον	παιδευσαμένην	παιδευσάμενον

Plural

Nom.	παιδευσάμενοι	παιδευσάμεναι	παιδευσάμενα
Gen.	παιδευσαμένων	παιδευσαμένων	παιδευσαμένων
Dat.	παιδευσαμένοις	παιδευσαμέναις	παιδευσαμένοις
Acc.	παιδευσαμένους	παιδευσαμένας	παιδευσάμενα

Second Aorist Middle
Singular

	Masculine	Feminine	Neuter
Nom.	λιπόμενος	λιπομένη	λιπόμενον
Gen.	λιπομένου	λιπομένης	λιπομένου
Dat.	λιπομένῳ	λιπομένῃ	λιπομένῳ
Acc.	λιπόμενον	λιπομένην	λιπόμενον

Declensions

<u>Plural</u>

Nom.	λιπόμενοι	λιπόμεναι	λιπόμενα
Gen.	λιπομένων	λιπομένων	λιπομένων
Dat.	λιπομένοις	λιπομέναις	λιπομένοις
Acc.	λιπομένους	λιπομένας	λιπόμενα

Aorist Passive
<u>Singular</u>

	Masculine	Feminine	Neuter
Nom.	παιδευθείς	παιδευθεῖσα	παιδευθέν
Gen.	παιδευθέντος	παιδευθείσης	παιδευθέντος
Dat.	παιδευθέντι	παιδευθείσῃ	παιδευθέντι
Acc.	παιδευθέντα	παιδευθεῖσαν	παιδευθέν

<u>Plural</u>

Nom.	παιδευθέντες	παιδευθεῖσαι	παιδευθέντα
Gen.	παιδευθέντων	παιδευθεισῶν	παιδευθέντων
Dat.	παιδευθεῖσι(ν)	παιδευθείσαις	παιδευθεῖσι(ν)
Acc.	παιδευθέντας	παιδευθείσας	παιδευθέντα

Perfect Middle-Passive
<u>Singular</u>

	Masculine	Feminine	Neuter
Nom.	πεπαιδευμένος	πεπαιδευμένη	πεπαιδευμένον
Gen.	πεπαιδευμένου	πεπαιδευμένης	πεπαιδευμένου
Dat.	πεπαιδευμένῳ	πεπαιδευμένῃ	πεπαιδευμένῳ
Acc.	πεπαιδεύμενον	πεπαιδευμένην	πεπαιδεύμενον

<u>Plural</u>

Nom.	πεπαιδεύμενοι	πεπαιδεύμεναι	πεπαιδεύμενα
Gen.	πεπαιδευμένων	πεπαιδευμένων	πεπαιδευμένων
Dat.	πεπαιδευμένοις	πεπαιδευμέναις	πεπαιδευμένοις
Acc.	πεπαιδευμένους	πεπαιδευμένας	πεπαιδεύμενα

<u>Pronouns</u>

1st & 2nd Person Personal

First Person		Second Person	
<u>Singular</u>	<u>Plural</u>	<u>Singular</u>	<u>Plural</u>
ἐγώ	ἡμεῖς	σύ	ὑμεῖς
ἐμοῦ (μου)	ἡμῶν	σοῦ (σου)	ὑμῶν
ἐμοί (μοι)	ἡμῖν	σοί (σοι)	ὑμῖν
ἐμέ (με)	ἡμᾶς	σέ (σε)	ὑμᾶς

Declensions

3rd Person Personal/Intensive/Identifying

	Singular			Plural		
	Masculine	Feminine	Neuter	Masculine	Feminine	Neuter
Nom.	αὐτός	αὐτή	αὐτό	αὐτοί	αὐταί	αὐτά
Gen.	αὐτοῦ	αὐτῆς	αὐτοῦ	αὐτῶν	αὐτῶν	αὐτῶν
Dat.	αὐτῷ	αὐτῇ	αὐτῷ	αὐτοῖς	αὐταῖς	αὐτοῖς
Acc.	αὐτόν	αὐτήν	αὐτό	αὐτούς	αὐτάς	αὐτά

Demonstratives

	Singular			Plural		
	Masculine	Feminine	Neuter	Masculine	Feminine	Neuter
Nom.	ἐκεῖνος	ἐκείνη	ἐκεῖνο	ἐκεῖνοι	ἐκεῖναι	ἐκεῖνα
Gen.	ἐκείνου	ἐκείνης	ἐκείνου	ἐκείνων	ἐκείνων	ἐκείνων
Dat.	ἐκείνῳ	ἐκείνῃ	ἐκείνῳ	ἐκείνοις	ἐκείναις	ἐκείνοις
Acc.	ἐκεῖνον	ἐκείνην	ἐκεῖνο	ἐκείνους	ἐκείνας	ἐκεῖνα

	Singular			Plural		
	Masculine	Feminine	Neuter	Masculine	Feminine	Neuter
Nom.	οὗτος	αὕτη	τοῦτο	οὗτοι	αὗται	ταῦτα
Gen.	τούτου	ταύτης	τούτου	τούτων	τούτων	τούτων
Dat.	τούτῳ	ταύτῃ	τούτῳ	τούτοις	ταύταις	τούτοις
Acc.	τοῦτον	ταύτην	τοῦτο	τούτους	ταύτας	ταῦτα

	Singular			Plural		
	Masculine	Feminine	Neuter	Masculine	Feminine	Neuter
Nom.	ὅδε	ἥδε	τόδε	οἵδε	αἵδε	τάδε
Gen.	τοῦδε	τῆσδε	τοῦδε	τῶνδε	τῶνδε	τῶνδε
Dat.	τῷδε	τῇδε	τῷδε	τοῖσδε	ταῖσδε	τοῖσδε
Acc.	τόνδε	τήνδε	τόδε	τούσδε	τάσδε	τάδε

ω-Verbs

Present Stem = first principal part - ω

Indicative

Present Active			Present Middle-Passive		
Singular	Person	Plural	Singular	Person	Plural
παιδεύω	1	παιδεύομεν	παιδεύομαι	1	παιδευόμεθα
παιδεύεις	2	παιδεύετε	παιδεύει (-η)	2	παιδεύεσθε
παιδεύει	3	παιδεύουσι(ν)	παιδεύεται	3	παιδεύονται

Present Active (ε-contract)			Present Middle-Passive (ε-contract)		
Singular	Person	Plural	Singular	Person	Plural
ποιῶ	1	ποιοῦμεν	ποιοῦμαι	1	ποιούμεθα
ποιεῖς	2	ποιεῖτε	ποιεῖ	2	ποιεῖσθε
ποιεῖ	3	ποιοῦσι(ν)	ποιεῖται	3	ποιοῦνται

Present Active (α-contract)			Present Middle-Passive (α-contract)		
Singular	Person	Plural	Singular	Person	Plural
τιμῶ	1	τιμῶμεν	τιμῶμαι	1	τιμώμεθα
τιμᾷς	2	τιμᾶτε	τιμᾷ	2	τιμᾶσθε
τιμᾷ	3	τιμῶσι(ν)	τιμᾶται	3	τιμῶνται

Infinitive

Present Active	Present Middle-Passive
παιδεύειν	παιδεύεσθαι
Present Active (ε-contract)	Present Middle-Passive (ε-contract)
ποιεῖν	ποιεῖσθαι
Present Active (α-contract)	Present Middle-Passive (α-contract)
τιμᾶν	τιμᾶσθαι

Participle

Present Active	Present Middle-Passive
παιδεύων, -ουσα, -ον	παιδευόμενος, -η, -ον
Present Active (ε-contract)	Present Middle-Passive (ε-contract)
ποιῶν, -οῦσα, -οῦν	ποιούμενος, -η, -ον
Present Active (α-contract)	Present Middle-Passive (α-contract)
τιμῶν, -ῶσα, -ῶν	τιμώμενος, -η, -ον

ω-Verbs

Imperfect Stem = augment + first principal part - ω
Indicative

Imperfect Active			Imperfect Middle-Passive		
Singular	Person	Plural	Singular	Person	Plural
ἐπαίδευον	1	ἐπαιδεύομεν	ἐπαιδευόμην	1	ἐπαιδευόμεθα
ἐπαίδευες	2	ἐπαιδεύετε	ἐπαιδεύου	2	ἐπαιδεύεσθε
ἐπαίδευε	3	ἐπαίδευον	ἐπαιδεύετο	3	ἐπαιδεύοντο

Imperfect Active (ε-contract)			Imperfect Middle-Passive (ε-contract)		
Singular	Person	Plural	Singular	Person	Plural
ἐποίουν	1	ἐποιοῦμεν	ἐποιούμην	1	ἐποιούμεθα
ἐποίεις	2	ἐποιεῖτε	ἐποιοῦ	2	ἐποιεῖσθε
ἐποίει	3	ἐποίουν	ἐποιεῖτο	3	ἐποιοῦντο

Imperfect Active (α-contract)			Imperfect Middle-Passive (α-contract)		
Singular	Person	Plural	Singular	Person	Plural
ἐτίμων	1	ἐτιμῶμεν	ἐτιμώμην	1	ἐτιμώμεθα
ἐτίμας	2	ἐτιμᾶτε	ἐτιμῶ	2	ἐτιμᾶσθε
ἐτίμα	3	ἐτίμων	ἐτιμᾶτο	3	ἐτιμῶντο

Future Active/Middle Stem = second principal part - ω
Indicative

Future Active			Future Middle		
Singular	Person	Plural	Singular	Person	Plural
παιδεύσω	1	παιδεύσομεν	παιδεύσομαι	1	παιδευσόμεθα
παιδεύσεις	2	παιδεύσετε	παιδεύσει (-η)	2	παιδεύσεσθε
παιδεύσει	3	παιδεύσουσι(ν)	παιδεύσεται	3	παιδεύσονται

Liquid Future Active			Liquid Future Middle		
Singular	Person	Plural	Singular	Person	Plural
φανῶ	1	φανοῦμεν	φανοῦμαι	1	φανούμεθα
φανεῖς	2	φανεῖτε	φανεῖ	2	φανεῖσθε
φανεῖ	3	φανοῦσι(ν)	φανεῖται	3	φανοῦνται

Infinitive

Future Active	Future Middle
παιδεύσειν	παιδεύσεσθαι

Liquid Future Active	Liquid Future Middle
φανεῖν	φανεῖσθαι

Participle

Future Active	Future Middle
παιδεύσων, -ουσα, -ον	παιδευσόμενος, -η, -ον

ω-Verbs

Liquid Future Active   Liquid Future Middle
φανῶν, -οῦσα, -οῦν   φανούμενος,-η, -ον

First Aorist Active/Middle Stem = 3ʳᵈ principal part - (σ)α

Indicative

First Aorist Active

Singular	Person	Plural
ἐπαίδευσα	1	ἐπαιδεύσαμεν
ἐπαίδευσας	2	ἐπαιδεύσατε
ἐπαίδευσε(ν)	3	ἐπαίδευσαν

First Aorist Middle

Singular	Person	Plural
ἐπαιδευσάμην	1	ἐπαιδευσάμεθα
ἐπαιδεύσω	2	ἐπαιδεύσασθε
ἐπαιδεύσατο	3	ἐπαιδεύσαντο

Liquid Aorist Active

Singular	Person	Plural
ἔφηνα	1	ἐφήναμεν
ἔφηνας	2	ἐφήνατε
ἔφηνε(ν)	3	ἔφηναν

Liquid Aorist Middle

Singular	Person	Plural
ἐφηνάμην	1	ἐφηνάμεθα
ἐφήνω	2	ἐφήνασθε
ἐφήνατο	3	ἐφήναντο

Infinitive

First Aorist Active   First Aorist Middle
παιδεῦσαι   παιδεύσασθαι

Liquid Aorist Active   Liquid Aorist Middle
φῆναι   φήνασθαι

Participle

First Aorist Active   First Aorist Middle
παιδεύσας, -σασα, -σαν   παιδευσάμενος, -η, -ον

Liquid Aorist Active   Liquid Aorist Middle
φήνας,-νασα, -ναν   φηνάμενος, -η, -ον

Second Aorist Active/Middle Stem = 3ʳᵈ principal part - ον

Indicative

Second Aorist Active

Singular	Person	Plural
ἔλιπον	1	ἐλίπομεν
ἔλιπες	2	ἐλίπετε
ἔλιπε	3	ἔλιπον

Second Aorist Middle

Singular	Person	Plural
ἐλιπόμην	1	ἐλιπόμεθα
ἐλίπου	2	ἐλίπεσθε
ἐλίπετο	3	ἐλίποντο

Infinitive

Second Aorist Active   Second Aorist Middle
λιπεῖν   λιπέσθαι

ω-Verbs

Participle
Second Aorist Active   Second Aorist Middle
λιπών, -οῦσα, -όν   λιπόμενος, -η, -ον

Perfect Active Stem =   Perfect Middle-Passive Stem =
   4th principal part - (κ)α   5th principal part - μαι
Indicative
   Perfect Active   Perfect Middle-Passive
<u>Singular</u>   <u>Person</u>   <u>Plural</u>   <u>Singular</u>   <u>Person</u>   <u>Plural</u>
πεπαίδευκα   1   πεπαιδεύκαμεν   πεπαίδευμαι   1   πεπαιδεύμεθα
πεπαίδευκας   2   πεπαιδεύκατε   πεπαίδευσαι   2   πεπαίδευσθε
πεπαίδευκε(ν) 3   πεπαιδεύκασι(ν)   πεπαίδευται   3   πεπαίδευνται

Infinitive
   Perfect Active   Perfect Middle-Passive
   πεπαιδευκέναι   πεπαιδεῦσθαι

Participle
   Perfect Active   Perfect Middle-Passive
πεπαιδευκώς, -κυῖα, -κός   πεπαιδευμένος, -η, -ον

Pluperfect Active Stem =   Pluperfect Middle-Passive Stem =
   augment + 4th principal part - (κ)α   augment + 5th principal part - μαι
Indicative
   Pluperfect Active   Pluperfect Middle-Passive
<u>Singular</u>   <u>Person</u>   <u>Plural</u>   <u>Singular</u>   <u>Person</u>   <u>Plural</u>
ἐπεπαιδεύκη   1   ἐπεπαιδεύκεμεν   ἐπεπαιδεύμην 1   ἐπεπαιδεύμεθα
ἐπεπαιδεύκης   2   ἐπεπαιδεύκετε   ἐπεπαίδευσο   2   ἐπεπαίδευσθε
ἐπεπαιδεύκει(ν) 3 ἐπεπαιδεύκεσαν   ἐπεπαίδευτο   3   ἐπεπαίδευντο

Aorist Passive Stem =   Future Passive Stem =
   6th principal part - ν   6th principal part - augment -ν
Indicative
   Aorist Passive   Future Passive
<u>Singular</u>   <u>Person</u>   <u>Plural</u>   <u>Singular</u>   <u>Person</u>   <u>Plural</u>
ἐπαιδεύθην 1   ἐπαιδεύθημεν   παιδευθήσομαι 1 παιδευθησόμεθα
ἐπαιδεύθης 2   ἐπαιδεύθητε   παιδευθήσει (-η) 2 παιδευθήσεσθε
ἐπαιδεύθη   3   ἐπαιδεύθησαν   παιδευθήσεται 3 παιδευθήσονται

Infinitive
   Aorist Passive   Future Passive
   παιδευθῆναι   παιδευθήσεσθαι

Participle
> Aorist Passive
> παιδευθείς, -εῖσα, -έν

Greek-English Vocabulary

The numbers listed after each item refer to the lesson in which the Greek word first appears. A complete list of principal parts for all verbs is listed after the vocabulary sections.

ἀγγέλλω announce, report 27
ἀγορά, -ᾶς, ἡ market-place 7
ἄγω lead, bring 2
ἀδελφός, -οῦ, ὁ brother 3
ἀδικέω injure, wrong, do wrong (to) 17
ἀδικία, -ας, ἡ injustice, injury, wrong 17
ἄδικος, -ον unjust 9
ἀθάνατος, -ον immortal 9
Ἀθῆναι, -ῶν, αἱ Athens 14
Ἀθηναῖος, -ου, ὁ Athenian 13
ἀθροίζω collect 23
αἱρέω take, seize, capture; (mid.) choose 17
αἰτέω ask (for), demand 27
ἀκούω (+ gen.) hear, listen to 11
ἀλήθεια, -ας, ἡ truth 18
ἀλλά but 6
ἄν postpositive adverb (untranslatable) 13
ἀνήρ, -δρός, ὁ man, husband 22
ἄνθρωπος, -ου, ὁ man; human being 3
ἄξιος, -α, -ον (+ gen.) worthy (of) 9
ἀπέχω keep away; (+ gen.) be away (from); (mid.) abstain from (+ gen.) 25
ἀπό (+ gen.) from, away from 4
ἀποθνῄσκω die, be killed 17
ἀποκτείνω kill 17
ἀρετή, -ῆς, ἡ excellence, virtue 7
ἁρπάζω seize 23
ἄρχω (+ gen.) rule; (mid.) begin 11
ἄρχων, -οντος, ὁ ruler 27
ἀσπίς, -ίδος, ἡ shield 21
ἅτε (+ part.) since 28

αὐτός, -ή, -ό (3ʳᵈ person pronoun); -self; same 16
ἀφικνέομαι (with εἰς or ἐπί + acc.) arrive (in/at), reach 24

βάλλω throw, hit 23
βασιλεύς, -έως, ὁ king 22
βιβλίον, -ου, τό book 5
βίος, -ου, ὁ life 4
βλάπτω harm, hurt 2
βουλεύω plan; (mid.) deliberate 11
βούλομαι want, prefer 25

γάρ for 6
γένος, -ους, τό race, birth 24
γέρων, -οντος, ὁ old man 21
γέφυρα, -ας, ἡ bridge 18
γῆ, γῆς, ἡ earth, land, ground, country 29
γίγνομαι become; be; happen; prove to be; be born 14
γνώμη, -ης, ἡ thought, opinion, judgment 7
γράφω write 2
γυνή, γυναικός, ἡ woman, wife 21

δέ and; but 6
δεῖ (+ acc. & infin.) it is necessary, must, ought 28
δεινός, -ή, -όν fearful, terrible, clever 9
δέκα ten 25
δέομαι (+ gen.) ask; need 29
δεσπότης, -ου, ὁ master, ruler 18
δέχομαι receive, accept 12
δή in fact, actually 23
διά (+ gen.) through (+ acc.) on account of, because of 8

διαβολή, -ῆς, ἡ prejudice, slander 7

διαφθείρω corrupt, ruin 2 & 17

διδάσκω teach 14

δίκαιος, -α, -ον just 9

δικαστής, -οῦ, ὁ judge; juror 18

δίκη, -ης, ἡ justice; court, case 7

διώκω pursue; prosecute 16

δῶρον, -ου, τό gift 5

ἐγώ I; ἡμεῖς we 16

ἐθέλω wish, be willing 2

εἰ if 13

εἰμί be 14

εἰρήνη, -ης, ἡ peace 7

εἰς (+ acc.) into, to 4

ἐκ (ἐξ) (+ gen.) out of, from 13

ἐκεῖνος, -η, -ο that 12

Ἕλλην, Ἕλληνος, ὁ a Greek 21

ἐν (+ dat.) in on, among 4

ἐνταῦθα (adverb) there, in that place, to that place; here; then 29

ἔξεστι(ν) (+ dat.) it is possible 16

ἐπαινέω praise, approve 24

ἐπεί, ἐπειδή when, since 12

ἐπί (+ gen.) on, upon; in the time of (+ dat.) at, by; for the purpose of
(+ acc.) to, toward; against (in hostile sense) 19

ἐπιβουλεύω (+ dat.) plot against 29

ἐπιλανθάνομαι (+ gen.) forget 29

ἐπιμελέομαι (+ gen.) take care (of), care for 35

ἕπομαι (+ dat.) follow 12

ἔρχομαι come; go 11

ἔτος, -ους, τό year 25

εὖ well 14

εὖ πράττειν (to) fare well 14

εὑρίσκω find 28

ἐχθρός, -οῦ, ὁ (personal) enemy 27

ἐχθρός, -ά, -όν hostile 27

ἔχειν χάριν thank, give thanks (to), feel grateful 21

ἔχω have 5; (+ infin.) be able, can 16

ἕως as long as, until 12

ζητέω seek, search for 23

ἤ or, than 25

ἤ . . . ἤ either . . . or 25

ἥδομαι (+ dat.) be pleased (with) 25

ἥλιος, -ου, ὁ sun 8

ἡμέρα, -ας, ἡ day 25

θάλαττα, -ης, ἡ sea 18

θάνατος, -ου, ὁ death 3

θάπτω bury 13

θεός, -οῦ, ὁ god 3

θυγάτηρ, -τρός, ἡ daughter 22

θύω sacrifice 24

ἰατρός, -οῦ, ὁ doctor 13

ἵππος, -ου, ὁ horse 3

καί and; even, also 3

καίπερ (+ part.) although 28

κακός, -ή, -όν bad, evil 9

κακῶς badly 14

καλέω call, summon; (pass.) be called (often with two nominatives) 27

καλός, -ή, -όν beautiful, fine, honorable, handsome 9

κατά (+ gen.) down from; down under; against
(acc.) down along; throughout; according to; opposite; by (distrib.) 29

κατηγορέω (+ gen. & acc.) accuse 17

κατηγορία, -ας, ἡ accusation 17

κατήγορος, -ου, ὁ accuser 17

κελεύω order, command 6

κέρδος, -ους, τό gain, profit 22

κῆρυξ, -υκος, ὁ herald 20
κίνδυνος, -ου, ὁ danger 5
κλέπτω steal 2
κλώψ, κλωπός, ὁ thief 20
κρίνω judge 23
κτάομαι acquire 24
κωλύω hinder, prevent 16

λαμβάνω take, seize; receive 11
λανθάνω (+ part.) escape the notice
   of 29
λέγω say, speak 4
λείπω leave 4
λίθος, -ου, ὁ stone 6
λόγος, -ου, ὁ word; speech; reason
   3
λύω destroy, release, set free; (mid.)
   ransom 8

μᾶλλον rather, more 25
μέγας, μεγάλη, μέγα large, great
   9
μέλλω (+ fut. infin.) be about (to),
   intend (to), be likely (to), be
   going (to) 6
μέμφομαι blame, find fault with
   16
μένω remain, stay, wait (for) 23
μετά (+ gen.) with; (+ acc.) after 8
μή not 13, 16
μήτηρ, -τρός, ἡ mother 22
μοῖρα, -ας, ἡ fate, destiny, portion
   18

ναῦς, νεώς, ἡ ship 22
νεανίας, -ου, ὁ young man, youth
   18
νέος, -α, -ον young; new; strange
   11
νῆσος, -ου, ἡ island 5
νικάω conquer, win 19
νίκη, -ης, ἡ victory 13
νόμος, -ου, ὁ law, custom 13
νόσος, -ου, ἡ disease 5

ξένος, -ου, ὁ guest-friend, stranger
   13

ὅδε,ἥδε, τόδε this 12
ὁδός, -οῦ, ἡ road 5
οἰκία, -ας, ἡ house 7
οἶνος, -ου, ὁ wine 5
οἷός, -α, -όν τε εἶναι (+ infin.) be
   able, can 16
ὅλος, -η, -ον whole 25
ὄνομα, -ατος, τό name, reputation
   24
ὄντι, τῷ in fact, really, actually 28
ὁράω see 19
οὐ (οὐκ, οὐχ) not 3
οὔποτε (μήποτε) never 23
οὐρανός, -οῦ, ὁ heaven, sky 4
οὗτος, αὕτη, τοῦτο this 12
οὕτως (οὕτω) so, in such a way 19

παιδεύω educate 2
παιδίον, -ου, τό (little) child 5
παῖς, παιδός, ὁ, ἡ child, boy, girl
   23
παρά   (+ gen.) from (the side of)
   (+ dat.) at (the side of)
   (+ acc.) to (the side of);
   along (the side of); contrary
   to 14
παρασκευάζω prepare; (mid. –
   intrans.) make preparations 29
πάρειμι be present 27
παρέχω provide, furnish 7
πάσχω suffer 11
πατήρ, -τρός, ὁ father 22
πατρίς, -ίδος, ἡ fatherland,
   country 21
παύω stop 8; (mid.) cease 11
πεδίον, -ου, τό plain 24
πείθω persuade 5; (mid. + dat.)
   obey 11
πειράομαι try, attempt 19
πέμπω send 4
πέντε five 25

περί   (+ gen.) about, concerning
       (+ acc.) about, around   14
πιστεύω (+ dat.) trust   7
πλέω sail   29
πλοῦτος, -ου, ὁ wealth   6
ποιέω make, do   17
πολέμιοι, -ων, οἱ enemy   28
πολέμιος, -α, -ον hostile   28
πόλεμος, -ου, ὁ war   6
πόλις, -εως, ἡ city, city-state   22
πολίτης, -ου, ὁ citizen   18
πολύς, πολλή, πολύ much, (pl.)
    many   9
πορεύομαι go, march, proceed,
    advance   14
ποταμός, -οῦ, ὁ river   4
πρᾶγμα, -ατος, τό deed, act; (pl.)
    trouble   23
πράττω do; make; achieve   14
πρός   (+ gen.) in the presence of, in
    the sight of, in the name of,
    on the side of; like
    (characteristic of); by (agency)
    (+ dat.) near; in addition to
    (+ acc.) to , towards; with
    regard to; against   27
πρῶτος, -η, -ον first   9

ῥήτωρ, -ορος, ὁ speaker, orator
    21

σοφός, -ή, -όν wise   9
σπεύδω hasten, hurry   2
στάδιον, -ου, τό stade   25
στρατηγός, -οῦ, ὁ general   6
στρατιά, -ᾶς, ἡ army, expedition
    7
στρατιώτης, -ου, ὁ soldier   18
σύ you (sg.); ὑμεῖς you (pl.)   16
συμβουλεύω (+ dat.) advise; (mid.)
    consult (with), ask the advice of
    29
σύμμαχος, -ου, ὁ ally   13
σύν (+ dat.) with   19
σφάττω slay, kill   14

σώζω save, bring safely   8
Σωκράτης, -ους, ὁ Socrates   22
σῶμα, -ατος, τό body   24

τάττω draw up, station, arrange,
    assign   24
τε ... καί both ... and   14
τέλος, -ους, τό end, result,
    outcome   27
τέλος (adv.) finally, at last   27
τιμάω honor   19
τιμή, -ῆς, ἡ honor   8
τιμωρέω avenge; (mid.) punish, take
    vengeance on   28
τολμάω dare   19
τράπεζα, -ης, ἡ table; bank 18
τρέπω turn   12
τριήρης, -ους, ἡ trireme   22
τρόπος, -ου, ὁ character, way,
    manner   24
τυγχάνω (+ part.) happen; (+ gen.)
    gain, hit, meet   29
τῷ ὄντι in fact, really, actually   28

υἱός, -οῦ, ὁ son   3
ὑπισχνέομαι promise   17
ὑπό (+ gen.) by, at the hands of;
    under (+ acc.) under (motion)
    11

φαίνω show, reveal; (mid.) appear
    17
φείδομαι (+ gen.) spare   13
φεύγω flee, escape, avoid   11
φθόνος, -ου, ὁ jealousy, envy,
    hatred   17
φίλος, -ου, ὁ friend   3
φόνος, -ου, ὁ murder   28
φυλάττω guard   6

χάρις, -ιτος, ἡ favor, goodwill   21
χειμών, -ῶνος, ὁ storm, winter
    21
χράομαι (+ dat.) use; enjoy; treat;
    consult (an oracle)   19

χρῆμα, -ατος, τό thing; (pl.)
    things, property, money 22
χρόνος, -ου, ὁ time 4
χρυσίον, -ου, τό gold 8
χώρα, -ας, ἡ country, land 8

ψεύδω deceive; (mid.) lie 16
ψυχή, -ῆς, ἡ soul 8

ὡς (+ fut. part.) in order (to), so as
    (to) 27
    (+ part. except future) on the
    grounds that, as if 28
ὥστε that, so that; (+ infin.) as (to);
    so as (to); so that 19

English-Greek Vocabulary

able, be ἔχω 16
    οἷός 16
about (to), be μέλλω (+ fut. infin.)
    6
about περί (+gen. or acc.) 14
abstain from ἀπέχομαι (+ gen) 25
accept δέχομαι 12
according to κατά (+ acc.) 29
account of, on διά (+ acc.) 8
accusation κατηγορία, -ας, ἡ 17
accuse κατηγορέω (+ acc. & gen.)
    17
accuser κατήγορος, -ου, ὁ 17
achieve πράττω 14
acquire κτάομαι 24
actually δή 23
    τῷ ὄντι 28
addition to, in πρός (+ dat.) 27
advance πορεύομαι 14
advise συμβουλεύω (+ dat.) 29
after μετά (+ acc.) 8
against ἐπί (+ acc.) 19
    πρός (+ acc.) 27
    κατά (+ gen.) 29
allow ἐάω 33
ally σύμμαχος, -ου, ὁ 13
along παρά (acc.) 14
also καί 3
although καίπερ (+ part.) 28
among ἐν (+ dat.) 4
and καί 3
    δέ 6
announce ἀγγέλλω 27
another ἄλλος, -η, -ο 28
appear φαίνομαι 17
army στρατιά, -ᾶς, ἡ 7
around περί (+ acc.) 14
arrive (at) ἀφικνέομαι 24
as if (to) ὡς (+ part) 28
ask δέομαι (+ gen.) 29
ask (for) αἰτέω 27
as long as ἕως 12

at ἐπί (+ dat.) 19
    παρά (+ dat.) 14
Athenian Ἀθηναῖος, -α, -ον 13
Athens Ἀθῆναι, -ῶν, αἱ 14
at last τέλος 27
at the hands of ὑπό (+ gen.) 11
avenge τιμωρέω 28
avoid φεύγω 11
away, be ἀπέχω 25
away from ἀπό (+ gen.) 4

bad κακός, -ή, -όν 9
badly κακῶς 14
bank τράπεζα, -ης, ἡ 18
be γίγνομαι 14
    εἰμί 14
beautiful καλός, -ή, -όν 9
because of διά (+ acc.) 8
become γίγνομαι 14
begin ἄρχομαι (+ gen.) 11
birth γένος, -ους, τό 24
blame μέμφομαι 16
body σῶμα, -ατος, τό 24
book βιβλίον, -ου, τό 5
born, be γίγνομαι 14
both ... and τε ... καί 14
boy παῖς, παῖδος, ὁ 23
bridge γέφυρα, -ας, ἡ 18
bring ἄγω 2
bring safely σώζω 8
brother ἀδελφός, -οῦ, ὁ 3
bury θάπτω 13
but ἀλλά 6
    δέ 6
by ὑπό (+ gen.) 11
    ἐπί (+ dat.) 19

call καλέω 27
can ἔχω 16
    οἷός τε 16
capture αἱρέω 17
case δίκη, -ης, ἡ 7

cease παύομαι 11
character τρόπος, -ου, ὁ 24
child παῖς, παιδός, ὁ 23
child, little παιδίον, -ου, τό 5
choose αἱρέομαι (mid.) 17
citizen πολίτης, -ου, ὁ 18
city πόλις, -εως, ἡ 22
clever δεινός, -ή, -όν 9
collect ἀθροίζω 23
come ἔρχομαι 11
command κελεύω 6
concerning περί (+ gen.) 14
conquer νικάω 19
consult (an oracle) χράομαι (+ dat.) 19
consult (with) συμβουλεύομαι (+ dat.) 29
contrary to παρά (+ acc.) 14
corrupt διαφθείρω 2
country χώρα, -ας, ἡ
    πατρίς, -ίδος, ἡ 21
    γῆ, -ῆς, ἡ 29
court δίκη, -ης, ἡ 7
custom νόμος, -ου, ὁ 13

danger κίνδυνος, -ου, ὁ 5
dare τολμάω 19
daughter θυγάτηρ, -ρός, ἡ 22
day ἡμέρα, -ας, ἡ 25
death θάνατος, -ου, ὁ 3
deceive ψεύδω 16
deed πρᾶγμα, -ατος, τό 23
deliberate βουλεύομαι 11
demand αἰτέω 27
destiny μοῖρα, -ας
destroy λύω 8
die ἀποθνῄσκω 17
disease νόσος, -ου, ἡ 5
do πράττω 14
    ποιέω 17
do wrong (to) ἀδικέω 17
doctor ἰατρός, -οῦ, ὁ 13
down along κατά (+ acc.) 29
down from κατά (+ gen.) 29

down under κατά (+ gen.) 29
draw up τάττω 24

earth γῆ, -ῆς, ἡ 29
educate παιδεύω 2
either ... or ἤ ... ἤ 25
enemy πολέμιοι, -ων, οἱ 28
enemy (personal) ἐχθρός, -οῦ, ὁ 28
enjoy χράομαι (+ dat.) 19
envy φθόνος, -ου, ὁ 17
escape φεύγω 11
escape the notice of λανθάνω (+ part.) 29
even καί 3
evil κακός, -ή, -όν 9
excellence ἀρετή, -ῆς, ἡ 7
expedition στρατιά, -ᾶς, ἡ 7

fact, in δή 23   8
    τῷ ὄντι 28
faithful πιστός, -ή, -όν 38
fare badly κακῶς 14
fare well πράττειν εὖ 14
fate μοῖρα, -ας, ἡ 18
father πατήρ, -τρός, ὁ 22
fatherland πατρίς, -ίδος, ἡ 21
favor χάρις, -ιτος, ἡ 21
fearful δεινός, -ή, -όν 9
feel grateful χάριν ἔχειν 21
finally τέλος 27
find εὑρίσκω 28
fine καλός, -ή, -όν 9
first πρῶτος, -η, -ον
    πρῶτον (adv.) 33
five πέντε 25
flee φεύγω 11
follow ἕπομαι (+ dat.) 12
for γάρ 6
for the purpose of ἐπί (+ dat.) 19
forget ἐπιλανθάνομαι (+ gen.) 29
friend φίλος, -ου, ὁ 3
friend (guest-friend) ξένος, -ου, ὁ 13

from ἀπό (+ gen.) 4
　　ἐκ (+ gen.) 13
　　παρά (+ gen.) 14
furnish παρέχω 7

gain κέρδος, -ους, τό 22
　　τυγχάνω (+ gen.) 29
general στρατηγός, -οῦ, ὁ 6
gift δῶρον, -ου, τό 5
give thanks χάριν ἔχειν 21
go ἔρχομαι 11
god θεός, -οῦ, ὁ 3
going (to), be μέλλω 6
gold χρυσίον, -ου, τό 8
great μέγας, μεγάλη, μέγα 9
Greek Ἕλλην, -ος, ὁ 21
ground γῆ, -ῆς, ἡ 29
grounds that, on the ὡς (+ part.)
　　28
guard φυλάττω 6
guest-friend ξένος, -ου, ὁ 13

hands of, at the ὑπό (+ gen.) 11
handsome καλός, -ή, -όν 9
happen γίγνομαι 14
　　τυγχάνω (+ part.) 29
harm βλάπτω 2
hasten σπεύδω 2
hatred φθόνος, -ου, ὁ 17
have ἔχω 5
hear ἀκούω (+ gen.) 11
heaven οὐρανός, -οῦ, ὁ 4
herald κῆρυξ, -υκος, ὁ 21
here ἐνταῦθα 29
hinder κωλύω 16
hit βάλλω 23
　　τυγχάνω (+ gen.) 29
honor τιμή, -ῆς ἡ 8
　　τιμάω 19
honorable καλός, -ή, -όν 9
horse ἵππος, -ου, ὁ 3
hostile ἐχθρός, -ή, -όν 27
　　πολέμιος, -α, -ον 28
house οἰκία, -ας, ἡ 7

hurry σπεύδω 2
hurt βλάπτω 2
husband ἀνήρ, -δρός, ὁ 22

I ἐγώ 16
if εἰ 13
immortal ἀθάνατος, -ον 9
in ἐν (+ dat.) 27
in addition to πρός (+ dat.) 27
in fact δή 23
　　τῷ ὄντι 28
injure ἀδικέω 17
injury ἀδικία, -ας, ἡ 17
injustice ἀδικία, -ας, ἡ 17
in order (to) ὡς
intend μέλλω 6
in the name of πρός (+ gen.) 27
in the time of ἐπί (+ gen.) 19
into εἰς (+ acc.) 4
island νῆσος, -ου, ἡ 5

jealousy φθόνος, -ου, ὁ 17
judge δικαστής, -οῦ, ὁ
　　κρίνω 23
judgment γνώμη, -ης, ἡ 7
juror δικαστής, -οῦ, ὁ 18
just δίκαιος, -α, -ον 9
justice δίκη, -ης, ἡ 7

keep away ἀπέχω 25
kill σφάττω 14
　　ἀποκτείνω 17
killed, be ἀποθνῄσκω 17
king βασιλεύς, -έως, ὁ 22

land χώρα, -ας, ἡ 8
　　γῆ, γῆς, ἡ 29
large μέγας, μεγάλη, μέγα 9
last, at τέλος 27
law νόμος, -ου, ὁ 13
lead ἄγω 2
leave λείπω 4
lie ψεύδομαι 16
life βίος, -ου, ὁ 4

likely (to), be μέλλω 6
listen to ἀκούω (+ gen.) 11
little child, παιδίον, -ου, τό 5

make πράττω 14
       ποιέω 17
make preparations
       παρασκευάζομαι 29
man ἄνθρωπος, -ου, ὁ 3
       ἀνήρ, -δρός 22
man, young νεανίας, -ου, ὁ 18
many πολλοί, -αί, -ά 9
market-place ἀγορά, -ᾶς, ἡ 7
master δεσπότης, -ου, ὁ 18
meet τυγχάνω (+ gen.) 29
money χρήματα, -άτων, τά 22
more μᾶλλον (adv.) 25
mother μήτηρ, -τρός, ἡ 22
much πολύς, πολλή, πολύ 9
murder φόνος, -ου, ὁ 28
must δεῖ (+ acc.) 28

name ὄνομα, -ατος, τό 24
name of, in the πρός (+ gen.) 27
near πρός (+ dat.) 27
necessary, it is δεῖ (+ acc.) 28
need δέομαι (+ gen.) 29
never οὔποτε (μήποτε) 23
new νέος, -α, -ον 11
not οὐ (οὐκ, οὐχ) 3
       μή 13, 16
notice of, escape the λανθάνω (+
       part.) 29

obey πείθομαι (+ dat.) 11
old man γέρων, -οντος, ὁ 21
on ἐν (+ dat.) 4
       ἐπί (+ gen.) 19
on account of διά (+ acc.) 8
on the grounds that ὡς (+ part.) 28
opinion γνώμη, -ης, ἡ 7
opposite κατά (+ acc.) 29
or ἤ 25
orator ῥήτωρ, -ορος, ὁ 21

order κελεύω 6
other ἄλλος, -η, -ο 28
ought δεῖ (+ acc.) 28
outcome τέλος, -ους, τό 27
out of ἐκ (+ gen.) 13

peace εἰρήνη, -ης, ἡ 7
persuade πείθω 5
plain πεδίον, -ου, τό 24
plan βουλεύω 11
pleased, be ἥδομαι (+ dat.) 25
plot against ἐπιβουλεύω (+ dat.)
       29
portion μοῖρα, -ας, ἡ 18
possible, it is ἔξεστι (+ dat.) 16
praise ἐπαινέω 24
prefer βούλομαι 25
prejudice διαβολή, -ῆς, ἡ 7
preparations, make
       παρασκευάζομαι 29
prepare παρασκευάζω 29
present, be πάρειμι 27
prevent κωλύω 16
proceed πορεύομαι 14
profit κέρδος, -ους, τό 22
promise ὑπισχνέομαι 17
property χρήματα, -άτων, τά 22
prosecute διώκω 16
prove to be γίγνομαι 14
provide παρέχω 7
punish τιμωρέομαι 28
purpose of, with the avowed ὡς (+
       fut. part.) 27
pursue διώκω 16

race γένος, -ους, τό 24
ransom λύομαι 8
rather μᾶλλον 25
reach ἀφικνέομαι 24
really τῷ ὄντι 28
reason λόγος, -ου, ὁ 3
receive λαμβάνω 11
       δέχομαι 12
regard to, with πρός (+ acc.) 27

release λύω 8
remain μένω 23
report ἀγγέλλω 27
reveal φαίνω 17
river ποταμός, -οῦ, ὁ 4
road ὁδός, -οῦ, ἡ 5
ruin διαφθείρω 2
rule ἄρχω (+ gen.) 11
ruler δεσπότης, -ου, ὁ 18
    ἄρχων, -οντος, ὁ 27

sacrifice θύω 24
sail πλέω 29
same αὐτός, -ή, -ό 16
save σώζω 8
say λέγω 4
sea θάλαττα, -ης, ἡ 18
search for ζητέω 23
see ὁράω 19
seek ζητέω 23
seize λαμβάνω 11
    αἱρέω 17
    ἁρπάζω 23
-self αὐτός, -ή, -ό 16
send πέμπω 4
set free λύω 8
shield ἀσπίς, -ίδος, ἡ 21
ship ναῦς, νεώς, ἡ 22
show φαίνω 17
since ἐπειδή
    ἅτε (+ part.) 28
sky οὐρανός, -οῦ, ὁ 4
slander διαβολή, -ῆς, ἡ 7
slay σφάττω 14
so οὕτως (οὕτω) 19
Socrates Σωκράτης, -ους, ὁ 22
soldier στρατιώτης, -ου, ὁ 18
son υἱός, -οῦ, ὁ 3
so that ὥστε 19
soul ψυχή, -ῆς, ἡ 8
spare φείδομαι (+ gen.) 13
speak λέγω 4
speech λόγος, -ου, ὁ 3
stade στάδιον, -ου, τό 25

station τάττω 24
stay μένω 23
steal κλέπτω 2
stone λίθος, -ου, ὁ 6
stop παύω 8
storm χειμών, -ῶνος, ὁ 21
strange νέος, -α, -ον 11
stranger ξένος, -ου, ὁ 13
such a way, in οὕτως (οὕτω) 19
suffer πάσχω 11
sun ἥλιος, -ου, ὁ 8

table τράπεζα, -ης, ἡ 18
take λαμβάνω 11
    αἱρέω 17
teach διδάσκω 14
ten δέκα 25
terrible δεινός, -ή, -όν 9
than ἤ 25
thank χάριν ἔχειν 21
thanks, give χάριν ἔχειν 21
that ἐκεῖνος, -η, -ον 12
    ὥστε 19
then ἐνταῦθα 29
there ἐνταῦθα 29
thief κλώψ, -πός, ὁ 21
thing χρῆμα, -ατος, τό 22
this ὅδε, ἥδε, τόδε 12
    οὗτος, αὕτη, τοῦτο 12
thought γνώμη, -ης, ἡ 7
through διά (+ gen.) 8
throw βάλλω 23
time χρόνος, -ου, ὁ 4
time of, in the ἐπί (+ gen.) 19
to εἰς (+ acc.) 4
    παρά (+ acc.) 14
    ἐπί (+ acc.) 19
    πρός (+ acc.) 27
toward ἐπί (+ acc.) 19
    πρός (+ acc.) 27
treat χράομαι (+ dat.) 19
trireme τριήρης, -ους, ἡ 22
trouble πράγματα, -άτων, τά 23
true ἀληθής, -ές 23

trust πιστεύω (dat.) 7
truth ἀλήθεια, -ας, ἡ 18
try πειράομαι 19
turn τρέπω 12

under ὑπό (+ gen. or acc.) 11
unjust ἄδικος, -ον 9
until ἕως 12
upon ἐπί (+ gen.) 19
use χράομαι (+ dat.) 19

victory νίκη, -ης, ἡ 13
virtue ἀρετή, -ῆς, ἡ 7

wait (for) μένω 23
want βούλομαι 25
war πόλεμος, -ου, ὁ 6
way, in such a οὕτως (οὕτω) 19
wealth πλοῦτος, -ου, ὁ 6
well εὖ 14
when ἐπεί, ἐπειδή 12
whole ὅλος, -η, -ον 25
wife γυνή, γυναικός, ἡ 21
willing, be ἐθέλω 2

win νικάω 19
wine οἶνος, -ου, ὁ 5
winter χειμών, -ῶνος, ὁ 21
wise σοφός, -ή, -όν 9
wish ἐθέλω 2
with μετά (+ gen.) 8
     σύν (+ dat.) 19
with regard to πρός (+ acc.) 27
with the avowed purpose of (+ fut.
     part.) ὡς 27
woman γυνή, γυναικός, ἡ 21
word λόγος, -ου, ὁ 3
worthy ἄξιος, -α, -ον (+ gen.) 9
write γράφω 2
wrong ἀδικέω 17
     ἀδικία, -ας, ἡ 17

year ἔτος, -ους, τό 25
you (sg.) σύ 16
you (pl.) ὑμεῖς 16
young νέος, -α, -ον 11
young man νεανίας, -ου, ὁ 18
youth νεανίας, -ου, ὁ 18

Verb Principal Parts

ἀγγέλλω, ἀγγελῶ, ἤγγειλα, ἤγγελκα, ἤγγελμαι, ἠγγέλθην announce, report

ἄγω, ἄξω, ἤγαγον, ἦχα, ἦγμαι, ἤχθην lead, bring

ἀδικέω, ἀδικήσω, ἠδίκησα, ἠδίκηκα, ἠδίκημαι, ἠδικήθην injure, wrong, do wrong (to)

ἀθροίζω, ἀθροίσω, ἤθροισα, ἤθροικα, ἤθροισμαι, ἠθροίσθην collect

αἱρέω, αἱρήσω, εἷλον, ᾕρηκα, ᾕρημαι, ᾑρέθην take, seize, capture; (mid.) choose

αἰτέω, αἰτήσω, ᾔτησα, ____, ᾔτημαι, ____ ask (for), demand

ἀκούω, ἀκούσομαι, ἤκουσα, ἀκήκοα, ____, ἠκούσθην (+ gen.) hear, listen to

ἀπέχω, ἀφέξω (ἀποσχήσω), ἀπέσχον, ____, ____, ____ keep away; (+ gen.) be away from; (mid.) abstain from (+ gen.)

ἀποθνῄσκω, ἀποθανοῦμαι, ἀπέθανον, τέθνηκα, ____, ____ die, be killed

ἀποκτείνω, ἀποκτενῶ, ἀπέκτεινα, ἀπέκτονα, ____, ____ kill

ἁρπάζω, ἁρπάσομαι, ἥρπασα, ἥρπακα, ἥρπασμαι, ἡρπάσθην seize

ἄρχω, ἄρξω, ἦρξα, ἦρχα, ἦργμαι, ἤρχθην (+ gen.) rule; (mid.) begin

ἀφικνέομαι, ἀφίξομαι, ἀφικόμην, ____, ἀφῖγμαι ____ (with εἰς or ἐπί + acc.) arrive (in), arrive (at), reach

βάλλω, βαλῶ, ἔβαλον, βέβληκα, βέβλημαι, ἐβλήθην throw, hit

βλάπτω, βλάψω, ἔβλαψα, βέβλαφα, βέβλαμμαι, ἐβλάφθην (ἐβλάβην) harm, hurt

βουλεύω, βουλεύσω, ἐβούλευσα, βεβούλευκα, βεβούλευμαι, ἐβουλεύθην plan; (mid.) deliberate

βούλομαι, βουλήσομαι, ____, ____, βεβούλημαι, ἐβουλήθην want, prefer

γίγνομαι, γενήσομαι, ἐγενόμην, γέγονα, γεγένημαι, ____ become; be; happen; prove to be; be born

γράφω, γράψω, ἔγραψα, γέγραφα, γέγραμμαι, ἐγράφην write

δεῖ, δεήσει, δεήσει, ἐδέησε ____, ____ (+ acc. and infin.) it is necessary, must, ought

δέομαι, δεήσομαι, ____, ____, ____, ἐδεήθην (+ gen.) ask; need

δέχομαι, δέξομαι, ἐδεξάμην ____, δέδεγμαι, ἐδέχθην receive, accept

διαφθείρω, διαφθερῶ, διέφθειρα, διέφθαρκα, διέφθαρμαι, διεφθάρην corrupt, ruin

διδάσκω, διδάξω, ἐδίδαξα, δεδίδαχα, δεδίδαγμαι, ἐδιδάχθην teach

διώκω, διώξω, ἐδίωξα, δεδίωκα, ____, ἐδιώχθην pursue; prosecute

ἐθέλω, ἐθελήσω, ἠθέλησα, ἠθέληκα, ____, ____ wish, be willing

εἰμί, ἔσομαι, ____, ____, ____, ____ be

ἐπαινέω, ἐπαινέσομαι, ἐπήνεσα, ἐπήνεκα, ἐπήνημαι, ἐπηνέθην praise, approve

φείδομαι, φείσομαι, ἐφεισάμην, _____, _____, _____ (+ gen.) spare

φεύγω, φεύξομαι, ἔφυγον, πέφευγα, _____, _____ flee, escape, avoid

φυλάττω, φυλάξω, ἐφύλαξα, πεφύλαχα, πεφύλαγμαι, ἐφυλάχθην guard

χράομαι, χρήσομαι, ἐχρησάμην, _____, κέχρημαι, ἐχρήσθην (+ dat.) use; enjoy; treat; consult (an oracle)

ψεύδω, ψεύσω, ἔψευσα, _____, ἔψευσμαι, ἐψεύσθην deceive; (mid.) lie

Index